First World War
and Army of Occupation
War Diary
France, Belgium and Germany

23 DIVISION
68 Infantry Brigade
Durham Light Infantry
12th Battalion
8 February 1915 - 31 October 1917

WO95/2182/1

The Naval & Military Press Ltd
www.nmarchive.com
Published in association with The National Archives

Published by

The Naval & Military Press Ltd

Unit 10 Ridgewood Industrial Park,
Uckfield, East Sussex,
TN22 5QE England
Tel: +44 (0) 1825 749494

www.naval-military-press.com
www.nmarchive.com

This diary has been reprinted in facsimile from the original. Any imperfections are inevitably reproduced and the quality may fall short of modern type and cartographic standards.

© Crown Copyright
Images reproduced by permission of The National Archives, London, England, 2015.

Contents

Document type	Place/Title	Date From	Date To
Miscellaneous	This item has been conserved as part of the WO95/Digitisation Project Please Keep this sheet at the front of the box.		
Heading	WO95/2182/1 12 Bn Durham Light Inf Aug 1915-Oct 1917		
Heading	23rd Division 68th Infy Bde 12th Bn Durham Lt Infy Aug 1915-Oct 1917 To Italy.		
War Diary	Bramshott	24/03/1915	25/08/1915
War Diary	Ostrohove	26/08/1915	26/08/1915
War Diary	Houlle	27/08/1915	06/09/1915
War Diary	Hazebrouck	07/09/1915	07/09/1915
War Diary	Maison	08/02/1915	08/02/1915
War Diary	Blanche	09/09/1915	09/09/1915
War Diary	Estaire	10/09/1915	17/09/1915
War Diary	L'Hallobeau	18/09/1915	25/09/1915
War Diary	La Bassee Rd	26/09/1915	26/09/1915
War Diary	L'Hallobeau	27/09/1915	27/09/1915
War Diary	Estaires	28/09/1915	02/10/1915
War Diary	Trenches.	03/10/1915	07/10/1915
War Diary	Trenches 55/58	07/10/1915	07/10/1915
War Diary	La Rolanderie	08/10/1915	08/10/1915
War Diary	Trenches 55/58	12/10/1915	16/10/1915
War Diary	Bois Trenches	20/10/1915	20/10/1915
War Diary	Trenches 55/58	22/10/1915	23/10/1915
War Diary	La Rolanderie	25/10/1915	29/10/1915
War Diary	Trenches 55/58	30/10/1915	31/10/1915
Heading	23rd Division 12th D.L.I. Vol. 2 Nov 15 121/7635		
War Diary	Trenches I.263-I26.5 & I20.1	01/11/1915	02/11/1915
War Diary	La Rolanderie	03/11/1915	05/11/1915
War Diary	Trenches I.263-I 26.5 & I.20.1	06/11/1915	10/11/1915
War Diary	Bois Grenier Lines	11/11/1915	13/11/1915
War Diary	Trenches I 26. (305) I 20.1	14/11/1915	16/11/1915
War Diary	La Dormoire	17/11/1915	24/11/1915
War Diary	Rue Marle	24/11/1915	28/11/1915
War Diary	Trenches 62-66	29/11/1915	30/11/1915
Heading	23rd Div 12th D.L.S. Vol. 3 121/7935		
War Diary	Trenches 62-66	01/12/1915	02/12/1915
War Diary	Rue Marle	02/12/1915	07/12/1915
War Diary	Rue Marle & Trenches 62-66	07/12/1915	07/12/1915
War Diary	Trenches 62-66	08/12/1915	11/12/1915
War Diary	Rue Marle	12/12/1915	14/12/1915
War Diary	Jesus Farm	14/12/1915	22/12/1915
War Diary	Trenches I-31 (1-5) I.32	23/12/1915	26/12/1915
War Diary	Rue Delettree.	27/12/1915	30/12/1915
War Diary	Trenches I.31. (1-5) I.31	31/12/1915	31/12/1915
Heading	12th Durham L.I. Vol. 4 Jan (23)		
War Diary	I.31 (1-5) and I.32	01/01/1916	03/01/1916
War Diary	La Rolanderie	04/01/1916	07/01/1916
War Diary	La Rolanderie And Fort Rompu	07/01/1916	07/01/1916
War Diary	Fort Rompu	08/01/1916	15/01/1916

War Diary	Trenches I.15 (1-2) I.21 (3-4) I.16.	16/01/1916	19/01/1916
War Diary	Rue Marle	20/01/1916	23/01/1916
War Diary	Trenches I.21. (3-4) I.15 (1-2) I.16	24/01/1916	26/01/1916
War Diary	Trenches	26/01/1916	27/01/1916
War Diary	Rue Marle	28/01/1916	31/01/1916
War Diary	L'Hallobeau	01/02/1916	08/02/1916
War Diary	Trenches I.31 (1-5)	09/02/1916	12/02/1916
War Diary	Rue D'Lettree	13/02/1916	17/02/1916
War Diary	Trenches I.31 (1-5).	18/02/1916	21/02/1916
War Diary	Fort Rompu	22/02/1916	27/02/1916
War Diary	Morbecque	28/02/1916	29/02/1916
War Diary	Auchel	01/03/1916	08/03/1916
War Diary	Estree Cauchie	09/03/1916	15/03/1916
War Diary	Fosse 10	16/03/1916	20/03/1916
War Diary	Trenches Calonne Sector	21/03/1916	24/03/1916
War Diary	Bully Grenay	25/03/1916	28/03/1916
War Diary	Trenches Calonne Sector	29/03/1916	01/04/1916
War Diary	Calonne Cite	02/04/1916	05/04/1916
War Diary	Trenches Calonne Sect.	06/04/1916	17/04/1916
War Diary	Fosse 10	18/04/1916	26/04/1916
War Diary	Ourton	27/04/1916	05/05/1916
War Diary	Matringhem	06/05/1916	18/05/1916
War Diary	N.D. de Lorette. Sector.	19/05/1916	24/05/1916
War Diary	Souchez 2	25/05/1916	30/05/1916
War Diary	Bois-De-Noulette	31/05/1916	03/06/1916
War Diary	Trenches Souchez 2	04/06/1916	09/06/1916
War Diary	Bouvigny Woods.	10/06/1916	12/06/1916
War Diary	Deival	13/06/1916	13/06/1916
War Diary	Heuchin	14/06/1916	15/06/1916
War Diary	Reclinghem	16/06/1916	17/06/1916
War Diary	Reclinghem	18/06/1916	25/06/1916
War Diary	Picquigny	25/06/1916	29/06/1916
War Diary	Poulainville	30/06/1916	30/06/1916
Heading	68th Bde. 23rd Div. War Diary Brigade Temporarily Under Orders Of 34th Division 16th To 20th July. 12th Battalion. Durham Light Infantry. July 1916		
War Diary	Poulainville	01/07/1916	01/07/1916
War Diary	Fravillers	02/07/1916	02/07/1916
War Diary	Millencourt	03/07/1916	03/07/1916
War Diary	Trenches E.9.a.10.5 To E15.a.10.5	04/07/1916	04/07/1916
War Diary	Becourt Wood	05/07/1916	05/07/1916
War Diary	Trenches	06/07/1916	10/07/1916
War Diary	Albert	11/07/1916	15/07/1916
War Diary	Tara Trench	16/07/1916	16/07/1916
War Diary	Trenches	16/07/1916	17/07/1916
War Diary	Tara Trench	17/07/1916	19/07/1916
War Diary	Albert	20/07/1916	20/07/1916
War Diary	Franvillers	21/07/1916	26/07/1916
War Diary	Scott's Redoubt	27/07/1916	27/07/1916
War Diary	Contal Maison	28/07/1916	28/07/1916
War Diary	Sausage Valley.	29/07/1917	30/07/1917
War Diary	Becourt Road	31/07/1916	31/07/1916
Heading	23rd Division. 68th Brigade. 1/12 Battalion Durham Light Infantry August 1916		
War Diary	Becourt Road	01/08/1916	01/08/1916
War Diary	Shelter Wood	02/08/1916	02/08/1916

War Diary	Front Line	03/08/1916	04/08/1916
War Diary	O.9.Line No 2	05/08/1916	05/08/1916
War Diary	O.9. No. 2	06/08/1916	07/08/1916
War Diary	Becourt Road	08/08/1916	08/08/1916
War Diary	La Houssoye	09/08/1916	11/08/1916
War Diary	Ergine	12/08/1916	12/08/1916
War Diary	Eecke	13/08/1916	15/08/1916
War Diary	Steenwerck Area	16/08/1916	17/08/1916
War Diary	Armentiers	18/08/1916	24/08/1916
War Diary	Front Line Trenches	25/08/1916	30/08/1916
War Diary	Front Line Trenches 91/98	31/08/1916	31/08/1916
War Diary	Front Line91-98	01/09/1916	03/09/1916
War Diary	Nr Metteren	04/09/1916	05/09/1916
War Diary	Ouest Mont	06/09/1916	10/09/1916
War Diary	Moulien Au-Bois	11/09/1916	11/09/1916
War Diary	Millencourt.	12/09/1916	15/09/1916
War Diary	Becourt Wood	16/09/1916	18/09/1916
War Diary	Gourlay Trench	19/09/1916	22/09/1916
War Diary	Front Line	23/09/1916	26/09/1916
War Diary	The Dingle	27/09/1916	02/10/1916
War Diary	Gourlay Trench	03/10/1916	03/10/1916
War Diary	Crescent Alley	04/10/1916	06/10/1916
War Diary	O.G112	07/10/1916	07/10/1916
War Diary	Becourt Woods	08/10/1916	10/10/1916
War Diary	Ergnies	11/10/1916	13/10/1916
War Diary	Oneux	14/10/1916	15/10/1916
War Diary	Toronto Camp Poperinghe	15/10/1916	15/10/1916
War Diary	Zillebeke Bund	16/10/1916	16/10/1916
War Diary	Trenches	17/10/1916	20/10/1916
War Diary	Ypres	21/10/1916	23/10/1916
War Diary	Poperinghe	24/10/1916	29/10/1916
War Diary	Trenches	30/10/1916	31/10/1916
War Diary	Trenches (Dormy Ho)	01/11/1916	02/11/1916
War Diary	Bund	02/11/1916	05/11/1916
War Diary	Trenches	06/11/1916	09/11/1916
War Diary	Montreal Camp	10/11/1916	16/11/1916
War Diary	Barracks Ypres	16/11/1916	19/11/1916
War Diary	Trenches	20/11/1916	23/11/1916
War Diary	Barracks Ypres	24/11/1916	29/11/1916
War Diary	Montreal Camp	30/11/1916	07/12/1916
War Diary	Trenches Dorny Ho	08/12/1916	11/12/1916
War Diary	Ypres Hospice	12/12/1916	16/12/1916
War Diary	Trenches Dorny Ho	17/12/1916	20/12/1916
War Diary	The Bund	21/12/1916	23/12/1916
War Diary	Montreal Camp	24/12/1916	31/12/1916
War Diary	Trenches	01/01/1917	04/01/1917
War Diary	Infantry Barracks	05/01/1917	08/01/1917
War Diary	Trenches	09/01/1917	13/01/1917
War Diary	Infantry Bks	14/01/1917	16/01/1917
War Diary	Montreal Camp	17/01/1917	26/01/1917
War Diary	Trenches	27/01/1917	05/02/1917
War Diary	C Position	05/02/1917	09/02/1917
War Diary	Montreal Camp	10/02/1917	18/02/1917
War Diary	Trenches	19/02/1917	22/02/1917
War Diary	Barracks Ypres	23/02/1917	26/02/1917
War Diary	P Camp	27/02/1917	28/02/1917

Type	Description	From	To
War Diary	Houtkerque	01/03/1917	01/03/1917
War Diary	Merckeghem	02/03/1917	18/03/1917
War Diary	Herzeele	19/03/1917	21/03/1917
War Diary	L Lines	22/03/1917	28/03/1917
War Diary	D Camp A. 30.c.	29/03/1917	31/03/1917
Operation(al) Order(s)	Battalion Operation Orders No. 44	27/03/1917	27/03/1917
War Diary	D Camp A.30. (Cent)	01/04/1917	02/04/1917
War Diary	D Camp A.30. Sheet 28	03/04/1917	04/04/1917
War Diary	Sheet 28 Merckeghem	04/04/1917	14/04/1917
War Diary	Bradhoek Ypres	15/04/1917	18/04/1917
War Diary	Ypres Zillebeeke	19/04/1917	19/04/1917
War Diary	Zillebeeke	20/04/1917	23/04/1917
War Diary	Ypres	24/04/1917	27/04/1917
War Diary	Zillebeeke	28/04/1917	28/04/1917
War Diary	Zillebeke Trenches	29/04/1917	01/05/1917
War Diary	Steenvorde Area	02/05/1917	08/05/1917
War Diary	Steenvoorde & Montreal Camp	09/05/1917	09/05/1917
War Diary	Montreal Camp Hill 60 Centre	10/05/1917	10/05/1917
War Diary	Hill 60 Sub Sector	11/05/1917	13/05/1917
War Diary	Hill 60 Centre Subsection	13/05/1917	18/05/1917
War Diary	Montreal Camp	19/05/1917	27/05/1917
War Diary	Eecke	27/05/1917	30/05/1917
War Diary	Eecke & Railway Dugouts	31/05/1917	31/05/1917
War Diary	Railway Dugouts Near Ypres	01/06/1917	05/06/1917
War Diary	Ramparts Ypres	06/06/1917	06/06/1917
War Diary	Zillebeke Switch	07/06/1917	07/06/1917
War Diary	I.36.13.1.3. to I.36.c.2.5 (Sheet 28).	07/06/1917	08/06/1917
War Diary	I.36.13.1.3. to I.36.c.2.5 (Sheet 28). Battersea Farm.	08/06/1917	10/06/1917
War Diary	Battle Wood.	10/06/1917	14/06/1917
War Diary	Berthen Area	15/06/1917	26/06/1917
War Diary	Fletre (Sheet 27)	27/06/1917	30/06/1917
Miscellaneous			
Map	Map 14		
Miscellaneous	Map VI. To 23rd Division.		
War Diary	Micmac Camp Dickebusch	01/07/1917	31/07/1917
War Diary	Esquerdes	01/08/1917	13/08/1917
War Diary	Serques	14/08/1917	24/08/1917
War Diary	Cornwall Camp G.30.A.5.6	25/08/1917	27/08/1917
War Diary	Cornwall Camp	27/08/1917	29/08/1917
War Diary	H.26.B.5.8 Dickebusch Area	29/08/1917	31/08/1917
Miscellaneous	Operation Orders. by Lieut-Colonel R. Tyndall	15/08/1917	15/08/1917
Miscellaneous	Brigade 12th. Battalion The Durban Light Infantry.	21/08/1917	21/08/1917
Heading	War Diary Of 12th (S) Battalion, The Durham Light Infantry. From 1st Sept. 1917 To 30th Sept. 1917. Vol. 24		
War Diary	Dickebusch Area Camp at H26 b.5.8	01/09/1917	01/09/1917
War Diary	Micmac Camp A31.b.5.5. Sheet 25/NVI	02/09/1917	02/09/1917
War Diary	Steenvoorde Area	03/09/1917	04/09/1917
War Diary	Noordpeene	05/09/1917	13/09/1917
War Diary	Murrumbidgee Camp	14/09/1917	15/09/1917
War Diary	Hallebast Corner Camp	16/09/1917	19/09/1917
War Diary	In The Line	20/09/1917	25/09/1917
War Diary	Arragon Camp	26/09/1917	27/09/1917
War Diary	Ridge Wood Camp	28/09/1917	30/09/1917
Miscellaneous	12th. Battalion The Durham Light Infantry.	26/09/1917	26/09/1917
War Diary	Ridge Wood Camp	01/10/1917	02/10/1917

War Diary	Berthen Area	03/10/1917	03/10/1917
War Diary	Thieushouk Area	04/10/1917	15/10/1917
War Diary	Trenches E Of Polygone Wood	16/10/1917	16/10/1917
War Diary	Railway Dugouts	17/10/1917	22/10/1917
War Diary	St. Martin Au Laert	23/10/1917	31/10/1917

This item has been conserved as part of the WO95 Digitisation Project

Please keep this sheet at the front of the box

WO95/2182/1

12 Bn Durham Light Inf

Aug 1915 – Oct 1917

23RD DIVISION
68TH INFY BDE

12TH BN DURHAM LT INFY.
~~OCT~~ AUG 1915 - ~~FEB 1919~~
1917 OCT

To ITALY

WAR DIARY or INTELLIGENCE SUMMARY

Army Form C. 2118.

(Erase heading not required.)

Instructions regarding War Diaries and Intelligence Summaries are contained in F.S. Regs, Part II and the Staff Manual respectively. Title pages will be prepared in manuscript.

Place	Date	Hour	Summary of Events and Information	Remarks and references to Appendices
Bramshott	24/3/15	4 am	Advance Party M.G. Scott, Entrained Liphook Station for Southampton to Havre	a.D.&c
Bramshott	25/3/15	6 pm	1/2 Bn. Entrained at Liphook Station for Folkestone, embarked about 11.pm	a.D.&c
		7 pm	1/2 " " Reached Boulogne 1.am 26.3.15 marched to Rest Camp at Ostrohove	a.D.&c
Ostrohove	26/3/15	8 pm	Marched to Gare de Briques Station & entrained at about 10. am. joined by Advance Party & transport party en route for Houlle. Detrained at WATTEN about 3 am 27.3.15. Marched to Billets at Houlle, arriving at 5.45 am	a.D.&c
Houlle	27/3/15 to 5/5/15		Daily attention occupied in Divisional Brigade and Battn. Training and Specialist Section. 2nd Lt. R.V. Smith, H.N. Greenhalch, H. Heyes 3 days R.J. Cause unless Brigade M.G. Officer. 2nd Lt. G. Ostelhurston Proceeded to Hallow for Bailey Course	a.D.&c
Houlle	6/5/15	5.30 am	Marched by Road via St Omer, Argues to Billets at Hazebrouck	a.D.&c
Hazebrouck	7/5/15	8.5 am	do. Boore, Strazelle to Billets at MAISON BLANCHE. (HQrs. 65th July Brigade at Steenie)	a.D.&c
MAISON BLANCHE	8/5/15 9/5/15	3 pm	Battn. on instructor by G.O.C. 20th Division 20th Army Corps	a.D.&c
		10.30am	Marched to Billets at ESTAIRES attached to 60th Inft. Brigade for Instructional purposes in & out of Trenches. A&B Coys attached to 12 K.R.R in trenches for 24 hours. (1 Casualty)	a.D.&c
ESTAIRE	10/5/15	7.30am	C & D Coys marched to LEVANTIE attached to 12th K.R.R. occupied Trenches for 24 hrs. From about 6 p.m. (6 Casualties from R.G. wounds when leaving trenches)	a.D.&c

WAR DIARY
or
INTELLIGENCE SUMMARY.
(Erase heading not required.)

Army Form C. 2118.

Instructions regarding War Diaries and Intelligence Summaries are contained in F. S. Regs., Part II. and the Staff Manual respectively. Title pages will be prepared in manuscript.

Place	Date	Hour	Summary of Events and Information	Remarks and references to Appendices
Estaires	11/9/15	5 p.m.	Batt: Headquarters & trenches attached to 12th K.R.R. Remainder of Batt: in billets. One man accidently drowned in River Lys.	(A)
do	13/9/15	8.45 a.m.	A&B Coys attached to 12th K.R.R. & Oxon Bucks Regt in trenches near Laventie. One man gunshot wound after leaving trenches.	(A)
do	13/9/15	6.15 p.m.	Headquarters & C&D Coys occupies trenches near Laventie with 12th K.R.R. & Oxon Bucks Regt. 2 men wounded gunshot wound.	(A)
do	15/9/15	8.30 a.m. to 4.30 p.m.	A&B Coys working parties under R.E. at Fort Esquin & La Fleurbaix	(A)
do	17/9/15	2 a.m.	Batt: marched to billets at L'Hallobeau drawing 6 a.m.	(A)
Bailleul	18/9/15	6 a.m.	Working party of 400 men to La Creche under R.E. Batt: in reserve.	(A)
do	21/9/15	6.30 p.m.	200 men working party under R.E. at Rue Pluvis & La Creche.	(A)

Army Form C. 2118.

WAR DIARY
or
INTELLIGENCE SUMMARY.
(Erase heading not required.)

Instructions regarding War Diaries and Intelligence Summaries are contained in F. S. Regs., Part II. and the Staff Manual respectively. Title pages will be prepared in manuscript.

Place	Date	Hour	Summary of Events and Information	Remarks and references to Appendices
L'Hallobeau	22.23 24.25 Sept		Batt. in reserve.	(A)
La Bassée Rd	26/9/15	5.30 p.m.	Batt. marched to La Bassée Rd arriving there 9 p.m.	(B)
L'Hallobeau	27/9/15	2.15 p.m.	Batt. marched to billets at L'Hallobeau arriving 5 p.m.	(C)
Estaires	28/9/15	4 p.m.	Batt. marched to Rue Etaires & billeted at L'O.C.E. 2 Map 36a	(D)
do	1/10/15	6 a.m.	500 men working party at Sailly under R.E.	(E)
do	2.10.15	10 a.m.	Batt. marched to L'Hallobeau & in evening took over trenches from 8th Yorks. (Trenches 55-58)	(F)
Trenches	3rd 4th 5th 6th Oct		Batt. in Trenches – 1 man accidentally wounded from rear.	(G)

Army Form C. 2118.

WAR DIARY
or
INTELLIGENCE SUMMARY.
(Erase heading not required.)

Instructions regarding War Diaries and Intelligence Summaries are contained in F. S. Regs., Part II. and the Staff Manual respectively. Title pages will be prepared in manuscript.

Place	Date	Hour	Summary of Events and Information	Remarks and references to Appendices
Trenches 55/58	7.X.15	7.30 pm	Batts. relieved by XIII BTs. + marched to billets at La Rolanderie "B" Batt.	(PS)
La Rolanderie	8.X.15		200 men night working party on Ration + Tramway lines	(PS)
Trenches 55/58	12.X.15	6 pm	Batts. relieved XIII BTs. in trenches 55/58.	(PS)
do	13.X.15		1 man killed (gunshot wound, Barrie No 1 Platoon I 19.B. 8.5½) 1 man accidental gunshot wound L. Juligan 1 man drowning (believed wounded + drowning) Pte Bahit	(PS)
do	14.X.15		One man wounded G.S. wound	(PS)
do	16.X.15		Batts. relieved by XIII B.I.I. 2 Coys to Reserve Trenches in Bois Grenier Line + 2 Coys to billets in Rue de Lattre.	(PS)
Bois Grenier	20.X.15	6 pm	Relieved XIII BTs. in trenches 55-58. 1 man wounded accidental G.S. wound.	(PS)
Trenches 55/58	22.X.15			(PS)

1 McRae W. Ocey G. Dart A.P. Swft Lieut Colonel

WAR DIARY
or
INTELLIGENCE SUMMARY.
(Erase heading not required.)

Army Form C. 2118.

Instructions regarding War Diaries and Intelligence Summaries are contained in F. S. Regs., Part II. and the Staff Manual respectively. Title pages will be prepared in manuscript.

Place	Date	Hour	Summary of Events and Information	Remarks and references to Appendices
Trenches 55-58	23/4/15		1 man accidentally wounded. G.S. wound	(P)
La Rotonderie	24/4/15	7pm	Batt. relieved by 1st Sherwood Foresters & marched to Billets at La Rotonderie. Reserve D Batt.	(P)
do	26/4/15		200 men working parties Traceway Farm. 1 Casualty. G.S. wound	(P)
do	27.4.15		250 men do do	
do	29.4.15	7pm	Relieved 1st Sherwood Foresters in trenches 55/58	(P)
Trenches 55/58	30 & 31.5.15		Nothing to report. Very quiet	(P)

L.C. Shors Lieut Colonel
Comdg 12 (Ser) Bn Durham L.I.

12th Sept.
vol 2

121/7635

23rd Division

Nov 15

Q

Ack
ans.

Army Form C. 2118.

WAR DIARY
or
INTELLIGENCE SUMMARY.

(Erase heading not required.)

Instructions regarding War Diaries and Intelligence Summaries are contained in F.S. Regs., Part II. and the Staff Manual respectively. Title pages will be prepared in manuscript.

Place	Date	Hour	Summary of Events and Information	Remarks and references to Appendices
TRENCHES I.26.3-I.26.5 & I.20.1	1/4/15		Battalion in trenches, very quiet.	ADC
"	2/4/15		Nothing to report, very quiet. Relieved by 13TH D.L.I. Battalion marched to billets at LA ROLANDERIE ("D" Battalion.) Casualties 1 O.R. G.S.W. neck "A" Coy.	ADC
LA ROLANDERIE	3/4/15		Battalion in reserve.	ADC
"	4/4/15	6.15 P.M.	Working party BRIGADE TOOL DEPOT 100 men { 50 men from A Coy & 50 men from B Coy } Battalion in reserve.	ADC
"	5/4/15	6 P.M. 6.30 P.M.	Working party BRIGADE TOOL DEPOT 140 men { 70 men from C Coy & 70 men from D Coy } Carrying party SHAFTESBURY AVENUE 60 men from B Coy. Battalion in Reserve.	ADC
"	6/4/15	6.15 P.M.	Working party BRIGADE TOOL DEPOT 100 men { 50 men from A Coy & 50 men from D Coy } Battalion in reserve.	ADC
TRENCHES I.26.3-I.26.5 & I.20.1	6/4/15	7.15 P.M.	Relieved 13TH D.L.I. in trenches 55-58 or (I.26.3-I.26.5 & I.20.1).	ADC
"	7/4/15		Battalion in trenches, very quiet.	ADC
"	8/4/15		Battalion in trenches, very quiet. Casualties (1 O.R. wounded G.S.W. head)	ADC
"	9/4/15		Battalion in trenches, trenches 57-58 or (I.26.5 & I.20.1) & battalion headquarters were shelled between 8.45 A.M. & 9.15 P.M. about 10-12 rounds were fired at headquarters.	ADC
"	10/4/15		Battalion in trenches. Trench 57 or (I.20.1) & battalion headquarters were shelled (between 9.15 A.M. & 10 A.M.) Relieved by 13TH D.L.I. in evening trenches BOIS GRENIER & 2 Coy to billets. Two Coys to reserve trenches BOIS GRENIER & 2 Coy to billets RUE-DE-LETTREE.	ADC

WAR DIARY or **INTELLIGENCE SUMMARY.**
(Erase heading not required.)

Army Form C. 2118.

Instructions regarding War Diaries and Intelligence Summaries are contained in F. S. Regs., Part II. and the Staff Manual respectively. Title pages will be prepared in manuscript.

Place	Date	Hour	Summary of Events and Information	Remarks and references to Appendices
BOIS GRENIER LINES	11/XI/15		Battalion in Support. B A and D Coys in Support trenches. B.C. Coys in huts Rue-de-Lettree.	Do.
"	12/XI/15		Battalion in Support. A and D Coys in Support trenches. B.C. Coys in huts Rue de Lettree.	Do
"	13/XI/15		Battalion in Support. A and D Coys in Support trenches. B+C Coys in Billets Rue de Lettree. Relieve 13th Durham L.I. in trenches 55-58 & (I.20.3-I.26.5 and I.20.1). 10 Crack arrives for 24 hours instruction.	Do.
Trenches I.20.(3-5) I.20.1	14/XI/15		Battalion in Trenches very quiet. 10 Cadets left at 11-15 AM for " Bn. offr. spending the night in the trenches.	Do
"	15/XI/15		Battalion in the Trenches. Called upon Artillery for Retaliation at 2 pm	Do
"	16/XI/15		Battalion in Trenches. Relieved by 2/Northampton Regt. at 7-15 P.M. Proceeds to LA DORMOIRE.	Do
LA DORMOIRE	17/XI/15		Battalion at rest at LA DORMOIRE. Commences building OVENS.	Do

Army Form C. 2118.

WAR DIARY
or
INTELLIGENCE SUMMARY.
(Erase heading not required.)

Instructions regarding War Diaries and Intelligence Summaries are contained in F. S. Regs., Part II. and the Staff Manual respectively. Title pages will be prepared in manuscript.

Place	Date	Hour	Summary of Events and Information	Remarks and references to Appendices
LA DORMOIRE	18/XI/15		Battalion at rest at LA DORMOIRE. Furnished Working party of 100 men at LA VESSEE POST at 7 A.M. also working party at RUE MARLE at 7-15 P.M.	B. Dodds
"	19/XI/15		Battalion at rest at LA DORMOIRE. Furnished Working party of 100 men at RUE MARLE.	DO.
"	20/XI/15		Battalion at rest at LA DORMOIRE.	DO.
"	21/XI/15		Battalion at rest at LA DORMOIRE	ODC
"	22/XI/15	8 A.M.	Battalion at rest at LA DORMOIRE Working party Bois GRENIER LINE 200 men (50 men from each Coy.)	ODC
"	23/XI/15	8 A.M.	Battalion at rest at LA DORMOIRE Working party CORPS CALL DUMP 50 men from A Coy.	ODC
"	24/XI/15	9 A.M.	Battalion at rest at LA DORMOIRE Working party PT DU BIEZ 100 men	ODC
RUE MARLE	25/XI/15		Battalion moved from LA DORMOIRE (H.8.c.9.2) to "D" position RUE MARLE (H.6.d.7.4) ARMENTIÈRES.	ODC
"	26/XI/15			
"	27/XI/15		Battalion in reserve	

Army Form C. 2118.

WAR DIARY
or
INTELLIGENCE SUMMARY.
(Erase heading not required.)

Instructions regarding War Diaries and Intelligence Summaries are contained in F. S. Regs., Part II. and the Staff Manual respectively. Title pages will be prepared in manuscript.

Place	Date	Hour	Summary of Events and Information	Remarks and references to Appendices
RUE MARLE	28/7/15		Battalion moved from RUE MARLE into Trenches 62 — 66. Relieved 13th Durham L.I.	22.9
TRENCHES 62 – 66	29/7/15		Battalion in Trenches. Our artillery bombard German batteries; also Machine Gun opened fire at 5 p.m. on the placed which were bombarded by the Artillery.	A.B.
"	30/7/15		Battalion in Trenches. Enemy brought down a British Bi-plane in German line opposite Trench 63.	A.B.
"	31			

2353 Wt. W2514/1454 700,000 5/15 D. D. & L. A.D.S.S./Forms/C. 2118.

12 E 87 s!
tot: 3

D/7935

23

WAR DIARY
or
INTELLIGENCE SUMMARY. 2 h Bn. Durham Light Infantry

Army Form C. 2118.

Place	Date	Hour	Summary of Events and Information	Remarks and references to Appendices
TRENCHES 62-66	1/12/15		Battalion in trenches. Enemy very quiet. The 11th Northumberlands Fus.rs were on our right. The 8th Yorkshire Regt on our left. Map reference of Trenches. I.21.1 – I.21.2 – I.21.3 – I.21.4 – I.15.1 – I.15.2	7.9.
– do – and RUE MARLE	2/12/15		Battalion was relieved by 13th Durham Light Infantry. Battalion moved into Support. One Company in BOIS-GRENIER Line. One Company at CHAPELLE D'ARMENTIERES. Two companies and H.Q. at RUE MARLE.	7.9.
RUE MARLE	3/12/15		Battalion in Support.	7.9.
– do –	4/12/15		Battalion in Support. Provided Working Party of 40 men at Bde. HQS. "C" Company were heavily shelled by 4.7" H.E. about 4-15 p.m. – Losses about 4 hour. Casualties six killed and seven wounded.	7.9.
– do –	5/12/15		Battalion in Support. Very Quiet.	7.9.
– do –	6/12/15		Battalion in Support. Enemy shelled 'A' coy at CHAPELLE D'ARMENTIERES, about 3-30 p.m. No casualties.	7.9.

Army Form C. 2118.

WAR DIARY
or
INTELLIGENCE SUMMARY. 12th Durham Light Infantry.
(Erase heading not required.)

Place	Date	Hour	Summary of Events and Information	Remarks and references to Appendices
RUE. MARLE & TRENCHES 62-66	7/12/15		Battalion relieved 13th Durham Light Infantry in trenches (I.21.1.6.) I.21.1.4) (I.15.1-I.15.2) One man wounded. (self inflicted). Enemy very Quiet	T.D.
TRENCHES 62-66	8/12/15		Battalion in trenches. One man killed, shot through head whilst on sentry. Our Artillery very active during afternoon - cutting the enemy's wire.	T.D.
— do —	9/12/15		Battalion in trenches. Very heavy rain. Two men wounded, one shot through chest and the other through arm.	T.D.
— do —	10/12/15		Battalion in trenches. A very heavy Artillery duel. The enemy commencing at 9 a.m., we replied at 9.20. Duel lasted until 2.30 p.m. No casualties from shelling, but one man shot through head whilst observing Rifle Grenade firing. The Lincolnshire Regt. on our left and 11th. Northumberland Fus.rs on our right. The telephone wires were cut, so communication was kept up through us.	T.D.
— do —	11/12/15		Battalion in trenches. Very Quiet. We were relieved by 13th Durham Light Infantry. Moved into Reserve at RUE. MARLE.	T.D.

WAR DIARY
or
INTELLIGENCE SUMMARY. 12th Durham Light Infantry
(D. position R.E. Intrigue)

Army Form C. 2118.

Place	Date	Hour	Summary of Events and Information	Remarks and references to Appendices
RUE MARLE	12/12/15		Battalion in Reserve. Furnished working fatigue Parties. Also furnished 100 men for R.E. fatigue at 6.45 am.	N.S.
— do —	13/12/15		Battalion in Reserve — in Billets — furnished various fatigue Parties. Two Companies moved to new billets in ARMENTIERES — on the ERQUINGHEM Road.	N.S.
— do — and JESUS FARM.	14/12/15		The Battalion was relieved by the 1/WORSTERSHIRE Regt at 2 pm. The Battalion moving to Jesus Farm. Owing to floods the ERQUINGHEM BRIDGE was closed to traffic — the Battalion had to march via PONT DE NIEPPE. Battalion established in Billets at B.26.d.3.0.	N.S.
JESUS FARM	15/12/15		Battalion at rest in Billets at Jesus Farm. Furnished working party of 100 men for R.E. at 9 am. Also furnished party for presentation of Victoria Cross to Pte KENNY of 13th Durham Light Infantry.	N.S.
— do —	16/12/15		Battalion at rest in Billets at Jesus Farm. Furnished two fatigue parties for R.E. 100 men at I.19.c.27.2 and 100 men at I.19.c.6.2	N.S.

Army Form C. 2118.

WAR DIARY
or
INTELLIGENCE SUMMARY.   12th Durham L.I.

(Erase heading not required.)

Instructions regarding War Diaries and Intelligence Summaries are contained in F.S. Regs., Part II. and the Staff Manual respectively. Title pages will be prepared in manuscript.

Place	Date	Hour	Summary of Events and Information	Remarks and references to Appendices
JESUS FARM.	17/12/15		Battalion at rest at Jesus Farm. Furnishes fatigue parties for R.E. 100 men at 8 am at Point I.19.c.7.2. Also 100 men at 4-45 p.m. at I.19.c.7.2. Fatigue party of 1 Officer and 40 men at Bar. Hqs. at 9 am, Point N.W.a.6.1.	
-do-	18/12/15		Battalion at rest at Jesus Farm. Provides working party of 100 men at I.19.c.7.2 at 8 am. Also 20 men at 8 am at N.10.b.5.8.	do.
-do-	19/12/15		Battalion at rest at Jesus Farm. Provides working party of 100 men at I.14.d.3.9.	do.
-do-	20/12/15		at 5 pm. at I.14.d.3.9. Battalion at rest at Jesus Farm. Provides working party of 100 men at I.19.c.7.2 at 8 am.	do.
-do-	21/12/15		Battalion at rest at Jesus Farm. Zeppelin reported going North at 7-30 p.m.	do.
-do-	22/12/15		Battalion at Jesus Farm. Relieved 9th Bn. Yorkshire Regt in trenches I.31 (1-5) and I.32. Very quiet.	do.
Trenches I.31(1-5) I.32	23/12/15		Battalion in Trenches. Our Artillery bombards enemys wire and by Chapel. One man killed by Shrapnel.	do.

Army Form C. 2118.

WAR DIARY
or
INTELLIGENCE SUMMARY.
(Erase heading not required.)

2nd Bn. Durham Light Infantry

Place	Date	Hour	Summary of Events and Information	Remarks and references to Appendices
Trenches F31(c-s)F32	24/7/15		Battalion in trenches. Very wet. Our Artillery very active. The Germans opened very heavy Machine Guns and Rifle fire at 11 p.m. which lasted for about half an hour. The 2K.D.C.L.I. on our right and the Northumberland Fusiliers on left.	DS
—do—	25/7/15		Battalion in trenches. Very wet, many dugouts collapsing. Artillery very active.	Do
—do—	26/7/15		Battalion in trenches. The enemy's Artillery was very active. One officer killed by shrapnel. Relieved in the evening by the 2Bn. Durham Light Infantry, the Battalion moved to "C" position at RUE DELETTRÉE, one Company in Reserve at BOIS GRENIER.	Do
RUE DELETTRÉE	27/7/15		Battalion in "C" position. Provided Carrying Party of 20 men for R.E. at SHAFTESBURY AVENUE at 6 a.m. Also provided Working Party of 100 men for 2Bn. Durham L.I. in trenches at 5 p.m.	Do

Army Form C. 2118.

WAR DIARY
or
INTELLIGENCE SUMMARY.
(Erase heading not required.)

12th Durham Light Infantry

Place	Date	Hour	Summary of Events and Information	Remarks and references to Appendices
Rue Delettree	28/12/15		Battalion in "C" Position. Provides working party for R.E. at Shaftesbury Avenue at 8 am. Also furnishes working party of 100 men for 13th Bn. Durham Light Infantry in trenches at 6.30 am. Also same number at same place at 5 pm.	no.
Rue Delettree	29/12/15		Battalion in "C" Position. Provides same parties as previous day.	no
Rue Delettree	30/12/15		Battalion in "O" Position. Provides Carrying party to R.E. as before. Also furnished working party of 100 men for 13th Durham Light Infantry in the morning. Relieved 13th Durham Light Infantry, the Battalion moving to A position in trenches I.31 (1-6) and I.32.	C.P.S.

WAR DIARY
or
INTELLIGENCE SUMMARY.
(Erase heading not required.)

12th. Bn. Durham Light Infantry

Army Form C. 2118.

Place	Date	Hour	Summary of Events and Information	Remarks and references to Appendices
Trenches 7.51.c.1-6,12.d.1.	30/12/15		Battalion in trenches. The enemy were generally quiet except for short bursts of machine gun fire. Artillery very active on our right, during the morning. There were three accidental casualties about 1.0 p.m.	C.P.S.

L.C. Elwes Lieut Colonel
Comdg 12th Durham L.I.

19? Durham L.J.

1st 4 Tan

㉓

WAR DIARY
INTELLIGENCE SUMMARY.

12th Durham Light Infantry

Army Form C. 2118.

Place	Date	Hour	Summary of Events and Information	Remarks and references to Appendices
I.31(1-5) and I.32	1/7/16		Battalion in trenches. 11th Northumberland Fusiliers on our left and 7th K.O.Y.L.I. on our right. Our artillery and machine guns opened fire at 1.30 a.m. to cover a raiding party on our left. Enemy's artillery retaliated on our front and support trenches causing no damage. Otherwise the enemy were very quiet.	C.P.S.
do.	2/7/16		Battalion in trenches. Enemy shelled Headquarters and support lines heavily between 2 and 3 p.m. No damage was done otherwise they were quiet. Weather wet.	C.P.S.
do	3/7/16		Battalion in trenches. 7th D.C.L.I. on our right. Enemy bombarded Brewery Post about mid day. Three casualties. Relieved in evening by 13th Batt Durham Light Infantry, the battalion moving to 'D' position at LA ROLANDERIE	C.P.S.

Army Form C. 2118.

WAR DIARY
or
INTELLIGENCE SUMMARY.
(Erase heading not required.)

12th Durham L.I.

Place	Date	Hour	Summary of Events and Information	Remarks and references to Appendices
LA ROLANDERIE	4/16		Battalion in 'D' position. Provides working party of 40 men for R.E at SHAFTESBURY AVENUE at 8.45 am. also 150 men to work in front line trenches at 5 pm and 50 men to R.E at 7.30 pm at BOIS GRENIER CHURCH.	C.P.S.
do.	5/16		Battalion in 'D' position. Provided working party of 150 men to work in front line trenches at 8.30 am. also 40 men to R.E at 8.45 am. two working parties of 150 men to front line trenches at 5 pm and 50 men to R.E at 7.30 pm.	C.P.S.
do	6/16		Battalion in 'D' position. Provides working parties of 150 men to front line trenches at 8.30 am and 40 men to R.E at 8.45 am. Also further working parties 50 men to R.E at 2.15 pm, 150 men to front trenches at 5 pm and two parties of 50 and 30 men to R.E at 5 pm and 5.15 respectively	C.P.S.
do and Fort Rompu	7/16		Battalion in 'D' position. Provides working parties to work in front trenches of 150 men at 8.30 am also 40 men to R.E at 8.45 am. Battalion moved to FORT ROMPU at 4.45 pm, being relieved by 2nd Batt Northamptonshire Regiment.	C.P.S.

Army Form C. 2118.

WAR DIARY
or
INTELLIGENCE SUMMARY.
(Erase heading not required.) 12th Durham L.I.

Place	Date	Hour	Summary of Events and Information	Remarks and references to Appendices
Fort Rompu	8/16		Battalion at rest at Fort Rompu. Provided working party of three officers and 100 men for R.E. at Elbow Farm (H.29.4.c.1.3.) at 4.30 pm	C.R.S.
do	9/16		Battalion at rest at Fort Rompu.	D.O.
do	10/16		Battalion at rest at Fort Rompu.	D.O.
do	11/16		Battalion at rest at Fort Rompu. Provides the following Working Parties:- 50 men at 9 am at H.10.d. I.O. 100 men at 9 am at Fleurbaix H.21.d.9.3 70 men at 8 am at I.19.c.7.2. 70 men at 5-15 pm at Shaftesbury Avenue 70 men at 5 pm at Shaftesbury Avenue. 140 men at 5 pm at 3 Arm. X.	D.O.
do	12/16		Battalion at rest at Fort Rompu.	D.O.
do	13/16		Battalion at rest at Fort Rompu.	D.O.
do	14/16		Battalion at rest at Fort Rompu. Provides Working party 600 pm at Armentieres Dump.	D.O.

WAR DIARY or INTELLIGENCE SUMMARY

Army Form C. 2118.

Place	Date	Hour	Summary of Events and Information	Remarks and references to Appendices
B.H.Q. Fort Rompu	15/5/16		Battalion at rest at Fort Rompu. 300ft over trenches	DD
Trenches I.15(1-2) I.21(3-4) I.16.	16/5/16	I.15(1-2) I.21(5-4) I.16. 10pm	10th West Riding Regt. Battalion in trenches. Enemy very quiet during the night. Artillery active during the day.	DD
do	17/5/16		Battalion in trenches. The Northumberland fired in our right and the Somerset Regt on our left. One man killed and one man wounded - both whilst on sentry duty.	DD
do	18/5/16		Battalion in trenches. Very quiet.	DD
do	19/5/16		Battalion in trenches. The enemy's and our aeroplanes were very active during the day. A hostile aeroplane was hit and came down very carefully in the German lines. The Battalion was relieved by the 8th Durham Light Infy. Moves to E. Ralini. One Coy in support trenches, one Coy in reserve at Chapelle d'Armentieres & 2 coys in Rue	DD

Army Form C. 2118.

WAR DIARY
or
INTELLIGENCE SUMMARY. 12th Durham Light Infantry

(Erase heading not required.)

Instructions regarding War Diaries and Intelligence Summaries are contained in F. S. Regs., Part II. and the Staff Manual respectively. Title pages will be prepared in manuscript.

Place	Date	Hour	Summary of Events and Information	Remarks and references to Appendices
RUE MARLE	20th		Battalion in 'C' position. Provides the following working parties. 50 men at MINE AVENUE at 7-30 am. 100 men at MINE AVENUE at 5-30 pm	
– do –	21st		Battalion in 'C' position.	No.
– do –	22nd		Battalion in 'C' position.	No.
– do –	23rd		Battalion in 'C' position. Battalion relieved the 13th Durham Light Infantry in trenches I.21.(3-4). I.15.(1-2) & I.16. at 6-30 pm	No.
TRENCHES I.21.(3-4) I.15.(1-2) I.16.	24th		Battalion in trenches. Enemy very quiet. Artillery scheme by the O.C. 12th D.L.I. was carried out.	No.
– do –	25th		Battalion in trenches. The enemy and our aeroplanes were very active. The enemy firing at our aeroplane with rifle and M.G. fire.	No.
– do –	26th		Battalion in trenches. Enemy shell Battalion H.Q.s very heavily. Signal Dugt blown up. Killing five men. Keeps	D.

WAR DIARY
or
INTELLIGENCE SUMMARY

Army Form C. 2118.

12th Durham Light Infy.

Place	Date	Hour	Summary of Events and Information	Remarks and references to Appendices
Trenches (cont'd)	26/1/16		(cont'd) had to be moved temporarily. Enemy MGs very active	D.D.
TRENCHES	27/1/16		Battalion in trenches. Enemy again shelled Battalion Hqs. 8/Somerset Regt on our left & 10th Northumberland Fus. on our right. Battalion was relieved by 13th Durham L.I.	do
RUE MARLE	28/1/16		Battalion in Billets in D. position. Supplies working for R.E. 50 men at H.6.a.28 at 8.30 am. One company of the 15th Royal Scots were attached 16.12.A.D.L.1. for instruction.	do
-do-	29/1/16		Battalion in D. position. Supplies 50 men for R.E. 128/2 boy at 7-15 am. Another Coy of 15th Royal Scots attached 16 12A D2.1 for instruction	do
-do-	30/1/16		Battalion in D. position. 15 Royal Scots same company no on 28th attached for instruction. Supplies following working parties — 30 men for R.E. at 12-45 am 100 men for R.E at 2.30 am	do
-do-	31/1/16		Battalion in D. position. Moved into Brigade rest at L'HALLOBEAU at 5 pm. Two companies of the 15th Royal Scots billeted with us for one night	do

1.2.16.

R. Dawson Maj.
Commdg. 12 D.L.I.

WAR DIARY or INTELLIGENCE SUMMARY.

Army Form C. 2118.

12th Durham Light Infantry

Place	Date	Hour	Summary of Events and Information	Remarks and references to Appendices
L'HALLOBEAU	1/7/16	—	Battalion in Billets at L'HALLOBEAU. Two Companies of 1st ROYAL SCOTS left at 10 am for NEUVE BERQUIN. Provided working party of fifty men for 3rd Corps at N.16.b.2.9.	A.D. F/15
—do—	2/7/16	—	Battalion in Billets at L'HALLOBEAU. in Brigade Rest.	A.D.
—do—	3/7/16	—	Battalion in Billets at L'HALLOBEAU. Provided the following working parties. 160 men for R.E. at H.30.B.5.7 at 8 am. 160 men at I.14.B.8.6 at 5.30 pm 50 men at H.30.B.5.7 at 5.30 pm. 50 men at H.16.B.2.9 at 9 am. 80 men at I.19.C.6.2.	A.D.
—do—	4/7/16	—	Battalion at L'HALLOBEAU in Billets in Brigade Rest.	A.D.
—do—	5/7/16	—	Battalion at L'HALLOBEAU in Billets in Brigade Rest.	A.D.
—do—	6/7/16	—	Battalion at L'HALLOBEAU in Billets in Brigade Rest. Colonel returns from leave to England.	A.D.
—do—	7/7/16	—	Battalion at L'HALLOBEAU in Billets in Brigade Rest. Provided the following working parties. 160 men at H.30.B.5.7 at 8 am. 80 men at I.19.B.2.0 at 4 pm. 160 men at I.14.B.5.6 at 3.45 pm. 50 men at H.16.B.2.9 at 7.15 am	A.D.

WAR DIARY
or
INTELLIGENCE SUMMARY.

(Erase heading not required.)

12th Durham L.I.

Army Form C. 2118.

Place	Date	Hour	Summary of Events and Information	Remarks and references to Appendices
L'HALLOBEAU	8/2/16		Battalion in Billets at L'HALLOBEAU. Provides S/5 take over trenches at 5-0 p.m. Relieves 11th West Yorkshire Regt. in Trenches I.31.(1-5).	T.O.
TRENCHES I.31.(1-5)	9/2/16		Battalion in trenches. Very quiet. One man wounded. A Prussian Prisoner gave himself up ats trench I.31.2, having escaped from German lines about 11 p.m., afterwards discovered that he escaped from LILLE.	T.O.
-do-	10/2/16		Battalion in trenches. 11 Northumberland Fusiliers on our left and Yorkshire Regt on our right.	T.O.
-do-	11/2/16		Battalion in trenches. One man wounded. One Company of 25 North'd F.S. came into trench for instruction for one night.	T.O.
-do-	12/2/16		Battalion in trenches. We were heavily bombarded by enemy for three hours with H.E. Shells & Trench Mortars. Casualties 3 Killed. 16 wounded and 2 wounded in 25 N.F. Relieved by 13th Durham L.I. at 7 p.m.	T.O.
RUE D'LETTREE	13/2/16		Battalion in 'C' Provisional Rue D'LETTREE. Enemy Artillery very active. Provided following working parties. 50 men for R.E. at 1-30 p.m. 15 men for R.E. at 6-30 p.m.	T.O.

WAR DIARY
or
INTELLIGENCE SUMMARY. 1/2 Durham L.I.

(Erase heading not required.)

Army Form C. 2118.

Place	Date	Hour	Summary of Events and Information	Remarks and references to Appendices
RUE- D'LETTREE	14/2/16	—	Battalion in 'C' Position. Provides following Carrying Parties.	
			30 men at Bois Grenier at 7-45 a.m.	
			50 " " " " 1-30 p.m.	
			15 " " " " 6-30 p.m.	T/O
— do —	15/2/16	—	Battalion in 'C' Position. Our Colonel came for Instruction. Provides	T
			following Parties.	
			30 men at Bois Grenier at 7-45 p.m.	
			50 " " " " 1-30 p.m.	
			15 " " " " 6-30 p.m.	
			20 men for Transport lines L'EPINETTE. To drain Transport lines.	T/O
— do —	16/2/16	—	Battalion in 'C' Position.	T/O
do	17/2/16	—	Battalion in 'C' Position. — relieves 8th Durham Light Infantry in trenches I-31-(1-5) at 7-30 p.m. (Colonel for instruction left at 12 p.m.)	T/O
Trenches I.31-(1-5)	18/2/16	—	Battalion in trenches. Enemy very quiet.	T/O
— do —	19/2/16	—	Battalion in trenches. One officer wounded — 1 man killed & 2 wounded.	T/O

WAR DIARY
or
INTELLIGENCE SUMMARY.
(Erase heading not required.)

Army Form C. 2118.

2nd Durham Light Infantry

Place	Date	Hour	Summary of Events and Information	Remarks and references to Appendices
Tincles I.31-G-5	20/2/16	—	Battalion in trenches. Exceptionally quiet day.	nil
-do-	21/2/16	—	Battalion in trenches - Aeroplane activity. Relieved in evening by 16th Royal Scots 101st Bde. Battalion moving into Divisional Rest at Fort ROMPU.	nil
Fort Rompu	22/2/16	—	Battalion in Divisional Reserve at Fort ROMPU. Heavy fall of snow.	nil
-do-	23/2/16	—	Battalion in Divisional Reserve at Fort ROMPU. Enemy shelled near C Company Officers Billet. Very heavy delayed action H.E. shell, many did not explode. Battalion at Fort ROMPU. Test Gas Alarm at 11 p.m.	nil
-do-	24/2/16	—		nil
-do-	25/2/16	—	Battalion moved to BAILLY in Reserve to 8th Division.	nil
-do-	26/2/16	—	Left BAILLY, marched to MORBECQUE in Corps 1st Corps Rest.	nil
-do-	27/2/16	—	Battalion at MORBECQUE.	nil

Army Form C. 2118.

WAR DIARY
or
INTELLIGENCE SUMMARY.
(Erase heading not required.)

12th Durham Light Infantry

Instructions regarding War Diaries and Intelligence Summaries are contained in F. S. Regs., Part II. and the Staff Manual respectively. Title pages will be prepared in manuscript.

Place	Date	Hour	Summary of Events and Information	Remarks and references to Appendices
MORBECQUE	28/7/16		Battalion in Corps Rest at MORBECQUE.	T.D.
"	29/7/16		Battalion entrained for BRUAY – arrived in Bruay at Auchel at 6 p.m.	T.D.

J. C. Elers Irish Lt.
Comdg. 12th Durham L.I.

Army Form C. 2118.

WAR DIARY
or
INTELLIGENCE SUMMARY.
(Erase heading not required.)

12th Durham Light Infantry

Place	Date	Hour	Summary of Events and Information	Remarks and references to Appendices
AUCHEL	1/3/16	—	Battalion in Billets at Auchel – Bruay Area.	TNS
"	2/3/16			
"	3/3/16			
"	4/3/16		Battalion in Billets at Auchel. – Bruay Area.	TNS
"	5/3/16			
"	6/3/16			
"	7/3/16			
"	8/3/16			
ESTREE CAUCHIE	9/3/16		Battalion marched to Billets in Estree Cauchie.	TNS
"	10/3/16			
"	11/3/16			
"	12/3/16		Battalion in Billets at Estree Cauchie	TNS
"	13/3/16			
"	14/3/16			
"	15/3/16			
FOSSE 10	16/3/16		Battalion marched to Billets in Fosse 10. nr. Bully Grenay.	TNS
"	17/3/16		To "D" position in Cite Calonne. Lieut M.Firth wounded	TNS
"	18/3/16		Battalion in "D" position in Cite Calonne. Enemy M.G. guns.	TNS
"	19/3/16			
"	20/3/16			

Army Form C. 2118.

WAR DIARY
or
INTELLIGENCE SUMMARY. 12th Durham Light Infantry
(Erase heading not required.)

Instructions regarding War Diaries and Intelligence Summaries are contained in F. S. Regs., Part II. and the Staff Manual respectively. Title pages will be prepared in manuscript.

Place	Date	Hour	Summary of Events and Information	Remarks and references to Appendices
TRENCHES CALONNE SECTOR	21/3/16		Battalion took over trenches in "B" position from the 13th Batt. Durham Light Infantry. The 11th Northumberland Fus rs on our right and 2/Northampton Regt on our left. Enemy exceedingly quiet.	
	22/3/16		Battalion in Trenches. Enemy Trench Mortars very active	
	23/3/16		Battalion in Trenches. Heavy fall of snow. Enemy very quiet.	
	24/3/16		Battalion in Trenches. Fair amount of aircraft activity. Battalion was relieved by 13th Durham Light Infy in the evening - we moved to "D" position in Billets at BULLY GRENAY.	
BULLY GRENAY	25/3/16		Battalion in Billets at BULLY GRENAY. Provided daily fatigues for R.E.	
"	26/3/16		Battalion in Billets at BULLY GRENAY. Usual working parties.	

WAR DIARY
or
INTELLIGENCE SUMMARY.
(Erase heading not required.)

Army Form C. 2118.

12th Durham Light Infantry

Place	Date	Hour	Summary of Events and Information	Remarks and references to Appendices
BULLY GRENAY	27/6		Battalion in Billets in "D" positions in BULLY GRENAY	DD
"	28/6		Battalion in Billets in "D" position in BULLY GRENAY	DD
TRENCHES CALONNE SECTOR.	29/6		Battalion relieved 13th Durham Light Infy. in "B" position	DD
	30/6		Battalion in Trenches. 1st Batt. Blackwatch on our left the 11th Northumberland Fusiliers on our right. Enemy artillery fairly active. Great deal of air acft activity.	DD
"	31/6		Battalion in Trenches. Enemy artillery very active, firing about 1000 shells of various calibre between day break and noon. Poor air craft activity. Casualties three O.R. wounded.	DD

J.C. Elwes Lieut Colonel
Comdg 12th Durham L.I.

Army Form C. 2118.
Vol 7

XXIII

WAR DIARY
or
INTELLIGENCE SUMMARY. 12th Durham L. Infy
(Erase heading not required)

Instructions regarding War Diaries and Intelligence Summaries are contained in F.S. Regs., Part II. and the Staff Manual respectively. Title pages will be prepared in manuscript.

Place	Date	Hour	Summary of Events and Information	Remarks and references to Appendices
TRENCHES CALONNE SECT.	1/4/16	—	Battalion in trenches. Enemy's Artillery fairly active. Aircraft activity.	
CALONNE CITÉ	2/4/16		Battalion was relieved by 13th Durham L. Infy in "B" position. The Battalion proceeding to Calonne Cité "C" position. Provided usual R.E.	DO.
	3/4/16		Battalion in "C" position. Provided usual R.E. working parties.	DO.
	4/4/16		do.	DO.
	5/4/16		do.	DO.
TRENCHES CALONNE SECT.	6/4/16		Battalion relieved the 13th Durham L. Infy in "B" position	DO.
	7/4/16		Battalion in trenches. Enemy's artillery fairly active. Great deal of aircraft activity. 1 pt of Black Watch on our left. 1/10 North d'Suo on our right.	DO.

Army Form C. 2118

WAR DIARY
or
INTELLIGENCE SUMMARY 12th Durham L. Infy
(Erase heading not required.)

Instructions regarding War Diaries and Intelligence Summaries are contained in F.S. Regs., Part II. and the Staff Manual respectively. Title Pages will be prepared in manuscript.

Place	Date	Hour	Summary of Events and Information	Remarks and references to Appendices
TRENCHES CALONNE SECT	8/7/16		Battalion in trenches. Our artillery cut the enemy's wire in several places. Enemy's artillery unusually active	D.
	9/7/16		Battalion in trenches. We continued cutting enemy's wire during the morning. Aircraft activity on both sides	D
	10/7/16		Battalion in trenches. Weather fine. A previously organized sham attack was commenced at 1.30 p.m. all our Divisional artillery opening a continuous bombardment. Previous to this assembly trenches and jumping off places had been made. Our men enforced themselves in gas helmets during the early stages of the Bombardment. At 4 p.m. phosphorus bombs were thrown over the parapet and smoke candles were ignited & placed on the parapet. At this the enemy's artillery increased in intensity. At 4.30 p.m. "Zero" our artillery fire was intense forming a barrage on the	

WAR DIARY or INTELLIGENCE SUMMARY

12th Durham L. Infy.

Army Form C. 2118

Place	Date	Hour	Summary of Events and Information	Remarks and references to Appendices
TRENCHES CALONNE SECT.	11/4/16		enemy's front line. At 4.35 p.m. our artillery "lifted" onto the enemy's support trenches. At the same time the enemy also formed a barrage in front of our parapet, shells of every calibre were fired into our support trenches. The bombardment gradually ceased and at 5.30 normal conditions ensued. Enemy's artillery usually active the Battalion being relieved in the evening by the 13th Durham L. Infy. we proceeding to "D" position BULLY-GRENAY.	OO.
	12/4/16 13/4/16 14/4/16		Battalion at BULLY GRENAY "D" position. We provided the usual R.E. working parties.	OO.
	15/4/16		Battalion relieved the 13th Battalion Durham L. Infy in "B" position.	OO.

WAR DIARY
or
INTELLIGENCE SUMMARY

(Erase heading not required.) 12 Durham L. Infy.

Army Form C. 2118

Place	Date	Hour	Summary of Events and Information	Remarks and references to Appendices
TRENCHES CALONNE SECTOR	16/16		Battalion in trenches. The 1st Cameron Highlanders on our left the 10th North'd Fus on our right.	DD.
	17/16		Battalion in trenches. Artillery and aircraft activity on both sides.	DD.
	18/16		Battalion was relieved by the 13th Essex Regt we proceeding to FOSSE 10.	DD.
FOSSE 10.	19, 20, 21, 22, 23, 24, 25 4/16		Battalion at FOSSE 10. 400 men for R.E working parties furnished daily. Lieut Ashmenhayes wounded on the 23rd.	DD.
	26/16		Battalion marched to OURTON. the "rest area".	DD.
OURTON	27, 28, 29, 30 4/16		Battalion at OURTON. 350 men provided for RE working parties on the 29th.	DD.

J.C.Elwes
Lieut Colonel
Comdg 12 Durham L.I.

WAR DIARY
or
INTELLIGENCE SUMMARY

(Erase heading not required.) 1/2 d Durham Light Infantry

Vol 8   Army Form C. 2118

Place	Date	Hour	Summary of Events and Information	Remarks and references to Appendices
OURTON	1 5/16	—	Battalion at OURTON "the rest area"	DD.
	2 "		350 men provided for R.E. working parties on	DD.
	3 "		the 4th.	
	4 "			
	5 5/16	—	Battalion marched to MATRINGHEM.	DD.
MATRINGHEM	6 5/16	—	Battalion at MATRINGHEM. Practised "Company in attack".	DD.
	7 5/16	—	Practised Company in attack and rearguard. Musketry and bombing in the afternoon	DD.
	8 5/16	—	Half Battalion in attack and defence. Musketry and bombing in the afternoon	DD.
	9 5/16	—	Battalion in attack. Musketry and bombing in the afternoon	DD.
	10 5/16	—	Battalion in attack & rearguard. Musketry and bombing in the afternoon	DD.
	11 5/16	—	Battalion in attack and sighting line of defence. Musketry and bombing in the afternoon	DD.
	12 5/16	—	Brigade in attack. We were in the front line. Bombing in afternoon.	DD.

WAR DIARY
or
INTELLIGENCE SUMMARY (Erase heading not required.) 12th Durham Light Infantry

Army Form C. 2118

Place	Date	Hour	Summary of Events and Information	Remarks and references to Appendices
MATRINGHEM	13/5/16	—	Raining heavily. Company arrangements. Lectures on Interior Economy etc	D.D.
	14/5/16	—	Raining heavily. Company Lectures	D.D.
	15/5/16	—	Raining heavily in morning. Company lecture. Bombing and Company route march in the afternoon. We were in reserve Brigade in attack.	D.D. D.D.
	16/5/16	—	Battalion marched to PERNES-EN-ARTOIS entraining thence to BARLIN.	D.D.
	17/5/16	—	Baths in morning. Battalion in afternoon marched from BARLIN and relieved the 15th Battalion London Regt (Civil Service Rifles) in position NOTRE-	D.D.
N.D. de LORETTE. SECTOR.	18/5/16 19/5/16 20/5/16	—	DAME-DE-LORETTE Sector. Battalion in "6" position Artillery and aircraft activity on both sides. Battalion strengthening wire improving trenches occupied	D.D.

WAR DIARY or INTELLIGENCE SUMMARY

Army Form C. 2118

12th Durham Light Infantry

Place	Date	Hour	Summary of Events and Information	Remarks and references to Appendices
N.D. DE LORETTE SECTOR	21/5 22/5 23/5 24/5	— — — —	Battalion in "C" position. Unusual artillery activity. Enemy attack on the VIMY RIDGE on the night of the 21st. He gained 1600 yards of the British line. The division on our right counter-attacked on the night of the 23rd but failed in its objective. During the day the Battalion attacks on our Battalion's battle position took its frequently the battery's behind us. Red Guns were also received a and heavily shelled by Red Guns from the enemy's very a good deal of attention from the enemy's heavy artillery. Two officers and orderly room being left completely wrecked.	2@
SOUCHEZ 2	25/5		Battalion relieves the 13th Durham Light Infantry in "B" position. Being but relieved in position by the 10th Northumberland Fusiliers.	6@
	26/5		Enemy artillery shelled Arras Road; bombs exploding near Balonne. Read	10@
	27/5		Considerable aeroplane activity by our 'planes. Par Artillery shelled Vimy Ridge	10@

WAR DIARY or INTELLIGENCE SUMMARY

Army Form C. 2118

Place	Date	Hour	Summary of Events and Information	Remarks and references to Appendices
SOUCHEZ 2.	28/5/16		Rifle Grenade & Trench Mortar activity by both sides. Patrol from D Coy reconnoitred trench to German lines. (see 29/5/16).	D
	29/5/16		Bombardment by Germans of Bing Ridge about 12 nn. Patrol went out from D Coy & proceeded along trench from Snellback Trench. They threw bombs at German sentry post & into German Trench. Gained valuable information for which they have specially thanked in Brigade orders.	D
	30/5/16		Trench mortar and rifle grenade activity on both sides enemy being eventually silenced by a few rounds from our 4 gun trench mortar Battalion gun relieved by the 13th Durham Light Infantry and proceeded to "D" position nd huttments at BOIS-DE-NOULETTE.	D
BOIS-DE-NOULETTE	31/5/16		Battalion in "D" position nouvel R 8 working parties provided.	D

WMacdnys? Lt Colonel.
Cmdg 12th D.L.I.

WAR DIARY
or
INTELLIGENCE SUMMARY

Army Form C. 2118

XXIII

12th Durham Light Infantry

Place	Date	Hour	Summary of Events and Information	Remarks and references to Appendices
BOIS - DE - MOULETTE	1/6 2 3		Battalion in "D" position. Covered R.E. working parties supplying. Unusual activity on the part of our aeroplanes. Enemy's aeroplanes very quiet. The battalion stood to. S.O.S. in lit on the night of the 3rd on receipt of Message from the 13th D.L.I. who were being heavily shelled + whose telephonic communication was entirely cut. Battalion relieved the 13th Durham Light Infantry in "B" position SOUCHEZ 2. Enemy very quiet. A little shelling of the "ARRAS ROAD" took place during the relief.	PP PP
TRENCHES SOUCHEZ 2.	4/6		Battalion in trenches SOUCHEZ 2. Continual shelling of the whole sector. Considerable damage to our trenches in our left Coy.	P.S.
"	5/6		Battalion in trenches. Shelling of front line trench continues. One company of the ANSON BATTALION of the ROYAL NAVAL DIVISION came into trenches for instructions.	PP
"	6/6		Battalion in trenches. Shelling as usual, principally large Minenwerfer being used.	PP
"	7/6			

WAR DIARY
or
INTELLIGENCE SUMMARY

Army Form C. 2118

/12th Bn Durham Light Infantry

Place	Date	Hour	Summary of Events and Information	Remarks and references to Appendices
SOUCHEZ (Trenches)	8.6/16		Battalion in trenches. Slight Artillery activity on our front line. The Coy of the ANSON BATT was relieved by another Coy of the 1st West Riding Regt – we moving to BOUVIGNY WOODS	PD.
"	9.		The destruction from front line continues. Relieved by the 1st West Riding Regt – we moving to BOUVIGNY WOODS.	PD.
BOUVIGNY WOODS	10		Battalion in huts. Hostile aeroplane dropped bombs on Camp at 3. AM. No damage.	PD.
"	11		Battalion in huts in BOUVIGNY WOODS.	PD.
"	12		Battalion relieved at 1 pm by the 20th LONDON REGT., in marching to Billets at DEIVAL.	PD.
DEIVAL	13		Battalion marches to Billets at HEUCHIN.	PD.
HEUCHIN	14		Battalion in Billets at HEUCHIN.	PD.
"	15		Battalion marches to ROCKINGHAM. Billets. Complaints by the Brigadier on our march discipline.	PD.
ROCKINGHAM	16.		Interior economy & Battalion manoeuvres.	PD.
	17			

WAR DIARY or INTELLIGENCE SUMMARY

Army Form C. 2118

12th Bn. Durham Light Infantry

Place	Date	Hour	Summary of Events and Information	Remarks and references to Appendices
RECLINGHEM	18.6.16		Brigade Tactical Scheme. Battalion on left flank. Direction was East — the right Battalion was directing	DD
"	19		Divisional Tactical Scheme. 68th Bde on left. 69th Bde on right. On the centre battalion of the left Bde. Inter company sports held in the evening.	DD
"	20.		Battalion Drill in morning. Interior Economy in afternoon. Complete of inter coy. Sports in the evening.	DD
"	21.		Bde. Tactical Scheme. Attack on trenches — we were right Battalion very successful. Presentation of ribbons to men 68th Bde including Lt JB Jacques Mersey Coy 15+pt J & 21010 Pte + James att T.M. Batt the D.C.M.	DD
"	22.		Bde Tactical Scheme. Attack on trenches. we were left battalion	DD
"	23.		Bn resting.	DD
"	24.		Bn marched to AIRE station, entrained for the South and the train leaving at 10.26.	DD
"	25		Detrained at LONGEAU near AMIENS about 6 am + marched to billets at PICQUIGNY.	DD
PICQUIGNY.	26		Battalion resting in billets at PICQUIGNY.	DD

Army Form C. 2118

WAR DIARY
or
INTELLIGENCE SUMMARY
(Erase heading not required.)

12th Bn Durham L. Infantry

Instructions regarding War Diaries and Intelligence Summaries are contained in F.S. Regs., Part II. and the Staff Manual respectively. Title Pages will be prepared in manuscript.

Place	Date	Hour	Summary of Events and Information	Remarks and references to Appendices
PICQUIGNY	27/6 28/6 29/6 30		Battalion in billets at PICQUIGNY. Bn and Co. drill and route marches. Battalion left PICQUIGNY at 3.2.5 pm and marched to POULAINVILLE being established in billets there at about 7.15 pm.	DD DD
POULAINVILLE				

W M Melhuish Lt Colonel
Cmdg 12th D.L.I.

68th Bde.
23rd Div.

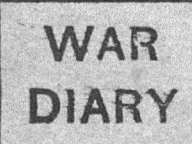

Brigade temporarily under orders
of 34th Division 16th to 20th July.

12th BATTALION.

DURHAM LIGHT INFANTRY.

JULY 1916

WAR DIARY or INTELLIGENCE SUMMARY

(Erase heading not required.)

2 Durham Light Infantry   Vol 10

Army Form C. 2118

Month of July 23

Place	Date	Hour	Summary of Events and Information	Remarks and references to Appendices
POULAINVILLE	1/7/16	—	Battalion resting in billets at Poulainville. Battalion left at 8.25 pm and marched to Fravillers.	DD.
FRAVILLERS	2	—	Battalion established in billets at Fravillers at 1.0 a.m. Left about 8.30 pm and marched to Bivouac at Millencourt arriving there about 12.0 midnight.	DD.
MILLENCOURT	3	—	Battalion in Bivouacs near Millencourt. Left about 5.0 p.m and marched to trenches along railway Albert - Dernancourt about E.9.d.10.5 to E.15.a.10.5. arriving about 9.30 p.m.	DD.
TRENCHES E.9.a.10.5 E.15.a.10.5	4	—	Battalion in trenches at E.9.a.10.5 to E.15.a.10.5. Battalion left at about 2.0 pm and marched to trenches and bivouacs in Becourt Wood at X.25.c central. Running heavily.	DD.
BECOURT WOOD	5	—	Battalion in trenches and bivouacs in Becourt Wood. Provided carrying parties the RE stores and rations for the Battalions on the 6.22% Brigade the Bombs, nations in the 6.22 Brigade the Battalion suffered about 4 casualties whilst doing this work called for 4 YORKS 8 pm to 3 a.m. Battalion left Becourt Wood taking over trenches from the 8th Yorks as follows.	
TRENCHES	6	—	"A" Co — BIRCH TREE AVENUE X.21.d.8-7 & X.22.a.4.6. "B" Co — Trenches X.21.b.3.9 - 5.4 - 8-6. "C" Co — Trench running from X.21.b.7.4 to X.22.a.0.4. "D" Co — The Triangle about X.15.d.5.1 to X.15.d.8.1. These trenches were deepened, firestepped and generally consolidated during the day and night. "D" Co were heavily shelled with whiz-bangs but no casualties were inflicted. "A" Co had two officers slightly wounded. Battalion was relieved by the 11th Northumberland Fusiliers and occupied trenches as follows.	Bn. Hd Quars X.21.d.2.4. DD.
	7	—	"A" Co. Relieved at 5 a.m. & proceeded to Aberdeen Avenue about X.26. "B" Co. Relieved at 2 a.m. & proceeded to trench parallel to the sunken road about X.21.d.3.0. "C" Co. Relieved at 12.30 a.m. & proceeded to trench running East from Willow Patch. "D" Co. Relieved at 5.30 a.m. & proceeded to trench X.21.d.29 - 5.6. Battalion moved up to support the 11th N.F's attack. "D" Co. ↑ climbed up about 9.30 a.m. via the triangle & advancing across the open from that "B" Co. ↓ position occupied and consolidated the triangle "D" Co X.15.b.8.2 - X.15.b.6.3 and B Co X.15.c.4.3 to X.15.c.8.8. "D" Co established a bombing post on the right flank against enemy strong post about X.15.b.8.2 and "B" Co established bombing posts on both sides of the trench occupied by them. This advance carried out above the open under	

WAR DIARY or INTELLIGENCE SUMMARY

Army Form C. 2118

12th Durham Light Infantry

Place	Date	Hour	Summary of Events and Information	Remarks and references to Appendices
	7/7/16	—	Heavy machine gun & rifle fire was made with the object of covering the flanks of the W/LTS and filling up the gap between them and the 11th M.F.S. "C" Co. about 1.30 p.m. advanced also their field advance across the open was exceedingly trying enfilade machine gun & rifle fire from CONTALMAISON but two platoons were eventually taken over by a covered way in the direction of X15 central and commenced digging in about X15.b.2/3. The remaining two platoons followed about 15 minutes later. "A" Co. began to help consolidate & clear the German trenches. During this consolidation three companies were much troubled by a group of enemy snipers from about X15.b.7.1/2 who caused many casualties. These snipers eventually silenced by one of our Lewis guns who opened fire on them. About this time they observed that there between about 12.30 p.m. sixteen were identified to digg but one platoon of "C" Co. was detailed with No 3 Platoon "A" Co. to reconnoitre Copse gully from the 24 Division. The 11th M.F.S. Lieut. Glencies with the MAJOR's party started running through BIRCH TREE AVENUE and the road running below PEAK WOODS and then the X16.d.51 5&X.16.9.24. By arriving at PEAK WOODS it was found that one was too dangerous to take a whole platoon along owing to the machine gun fire. This platoon was therefore halted with the Lewis gun in the road, and Lieut. Glencies with a Sergeant went on to reconnoitre almost immediately afterwards an immense number of Germans apparently to retire to small groups were seen in PEAK WOODS and others opened on the 2nd East Yorks & specially strongly within well 15 minutes of "A" Co. to rising line passed along Col. Y Molde Bayor said not to be presumed the Capt. and reported to Bn. Hd. Qrs. X14.b.2. 14 Plt. from the 17/11 advanced up the sunken road covered by our Lewis guns from about X15.d.8.9. to X15.d.8.9. & with No. 10 & 12 Plts successful in capturing 16 prisoners, but having withheld further advance & soon they counter-attacked there left behind, held by "A" Co. until dawn on the 8th being wounded at its time they began operations were carried out peaceably at establishing new line than that had no sleep this on about 40 hours in which had no sleep the "must" having all day. Two 2nd Lieuts. Count, Capt Banrest wounded & conditions being field obscured Colonel mission the whole pickets.	[88](?)
	8/7/16	—	"B" "C" & "D" Cos continued the shelling, devastation of the trenches. About X15.B.5.9 in the morning about X15.B.5.9. "B" "C" "D" Cos occupied by German strong post about X15.B.5.9 in the morning abandoned. BAILIFFS WOOD at dawn. Three companies were relieved by the W/LTS about 4 p.m. & and took to bivouacs in BECOURT WOOD via SAUSAGE VALLEY. Total casualties up to date 5 Officers, 156 OR.	[99](?)

WAR DIARY or INTELLIGENCE SUMMARY

Army Form C. 2118

12th Durham L. Infantry

Place	Date	Hour	Summary of Events and Information	Remarks and references to Appendices
Trenches	9/7/16		"A" Coy returned to Becourt Wood about 5 a.m. bringing in 9 prisoners, leaving 7 wounded during day all Coys rested, between 4 & 5 p.m. 3 Coys. "B" "C" & "D" moved to front but owing to enemy's artillery fire were obliged to wait until dusk before they could take up their line. 1,200 Bombs were carried up by "D" Coy. The Coys were disposed as follows. "C" Coy: (less 1 Platoon) assisted 13th D.L.I in consolidating trench at X.16.A.1.2 - X.16 C.1.9. & after doing considerable work ref'd to Becourt Wood about 1.am of 10th "B" Coy 2 Platoons assisted "D" Coy in holding road leading from Contalmaison 16.X.16.A.1.3. & mounted a party to hold ground commanding the 3 captured Field Guns & ammunition. a 3rd party held a detached post at X.16.a.3.8. the remainder held consolidated a trench at X.15.C.9.7 where it remained in support to front line. The 1 Platoon of "C" Coy was detailed to occupy & hold Baliff Wood "D" Coy occupied line X.16.A.1.2 to X.16.A.1.6. Their right joining with 13th D.L.I at dusk a party moved along trench at X.16.A.1.2 towards German line but were driven back by Enemy, a 2nd attack was made & the trench blocked at X.16.A.7.4 trench consolidated held by 2 platoons. During the night all parties consolidated trenches they were occupied by them. Casualties 1 Officers 2nd Lieut C.C. Longstaff wounded O. Ranks 1 killed & 7 wounded	C.E.C.

Army Form C. 2118

WAR DIARY
or
INTELLIGENCE SUMMARY
(Erase heading not required.)

12th Durham L. Infantry

Place	Date	Hour	Summary of Events and Information	Remarks and references to Appendices
Trenches	10/7/16		Positions of all parties unchanged. The platoons of "B" Coy at X.16.A.1.3. inflicted loss on Enemy during the morning by sniping & especially when enemy attempted a sortie from direction of Contalmaison wood, during afternoon enemy attempted twice to attack but on our extreme left but were driven back, about 3pm the 8th Yorks 69th Brigade took over our line & the 2 platoons of "B" Coy were sent back to Becourt wood which they reached about 4.30pm, it was found impossible to relieve the remainder owing to German machine gun & so they remained until after 4pm & then & owing to our heavy bombardment of Contalmaison the 2 Coy of 13 & whole of D. Coy were able to move back to Becourt wood without loss. The platoon of "C" Coy in Bailiff wood remained there until relieved at 11pm, they advanced by cross fire the advance of the 69th Brigade at 5pm against village of Contalmaison which village was taken by the 69th Brigade. The Batt = less 1 platoon of C. Coy moved to Albert about 9.pm & were billeted. Casualties. 1. Officer wounded. 2nd Lieut Duffy O. Ranks. 4 Killed - 3 missing - 7. wounded	G.E.C

Army Form C. 2118

WAR DIARY
or
INTELLIGENCE SUMMARY

(Erase heading not required.)

12th Durham Light Infantry

Place	Date	Hour	Summary of Events and Information	Remarks and references to Appendices
ALBERT	11/7/16		1 Platoon of C. Coy arrived Albert about 2 a.m. Battⁿ spent day in cleaning equipment etc & making good shortages. Odd German shells near billets.	C.E.C.
ALBERT	12/7/16		Battⁿ still at Albert. Coyˢ had inspections - more shelling round our billets - No casualties - O.R. 1 wounded.	C.E.C.
ALBERT	13/7/16		At Albert - Battⁿ inspected by C.O. German's shelled round billets during day & night no casualties. Heavy firing by our artillery at night.	C.E.C.
ALBERT	14/7/16		At Albert. Battⁿ to be ready to move at ½ hours notice. 15 n.c.m & 1 N.C.O working at Salvage Dump	C.E.C.
ALBERT	15/7/16		At Albert. Orders recᵈ about 3 a.m. for Battⁿ 68th Brigade to move to support 111th Brigade Battⁿ left Albert at 10 a.m. & moved to Tara Trench on left of Bapaume Road. & remained there during day & night.	C.E.C.
TARA TRENCH	16/7/16		Tara Trench. Battⁿ recᵈ orders during morning to relieve evening of 16th the 10th Loyal North Lancashire Regᵗ & move the Brigade was attached to the 34th Division from Mass. 4 the 10th North Lancashires were holding a line from X.4.C.4-12 through point 52 to wood S of point 62 to point 17-97 23.22 r.43. 4 Coyˢ were holding this front line the 2 Coyˢ on Left were in trenches but the 2 Coyˢ on R. were in a series of posts or shell holes & not connected up.	C.E.C.

Army Form C. 2118

WAR DIARY
or
INTELLIGENCE SUMMARY
(Erase heading not required.)

12th Durham L.I.

Remarks and references to Appendices

C.E.C.

Place	Date	Hour	Summary of Events and Information	Remarks
Trenches	16/7 con'd		The relief commenced at 7.30 p.m. & Coys moved in fours: order A.D.C. & B. 1 Platoon Coy. from each Coy had during afternoon visited H.Qrs of 10th Lancs & obtained particulars of line to be taken over, guides met Coys at Battn H.Qrs at Chalk Pit & about 10.30 pm the relief was completed & the new line taken over. A, D, & B Coys at once commenced digging assembly trenches about 100 yds in front of their line. C Coy worked on joining up b.J. & also the existing shell holes & posts they occupied. D Coy dug a communication trench from their original to the assembly trench, a small trench was dug from the wood S of 62 to front line.	
Trenches	17/7		17 The 13th D.L.I. who were to assist were unable to get to front line owing to shelling. Patrols were sent out during night but few enemy were located. Digging & consolidating original line continued during day without much shelling. 150 odd shells were fired on to the various parts of the line, at 10.30 am smoke barrage was fired but the enemy did not disclose his M.G. or free rifles. No very careful watch was kept, the only result being that enemy increased considerably his artillery fire on & behind the front line. The shelling was very heavy in Chalk Pit where Battn H.Qrs were stationed & about 4.30 pm owing to this very heavy shelling Battn H.Qrs was moved nearer to front line. At 5 pm orders came for the 12th D.L.I. to attack at 8 pm.	

WAR DIARY or INTELLIGENCE SUMMARY

Army Form C. 2118

12th Durham L.I.

Place	Date	Hour	Summary of Events and Information	Remarks and references to Appendices
TRENCHES	17/7/16		with the 13th D.L.I. in Support and the 1st Division on Right. The objective was the Enemy's trenches at X.4.C.7.4 to X.9.d.8.3. & when the 12th left their trenches the 13th would occupy the front line. If the attack was successful the 12th would Consolidate & hold the Captured trenches while the remainder of Brigade attacked Poizières. The attack was made in 2 waves of ½ Batt". A Coy. on Left & C. on Right. Supported by D & B Coys.	C.E.C
		8pm	At 8.pm the attack took place as ordered. The Stokes mortars were however falling about 50yds short & at 8.4pm the attackers were all going forward at this time the Enemys M.G. fire was intense. One platoon got to point X.10.B.2.9. but the Cross fire of M.G's. made any further advance impossible. D. Coy were only saved from annihilation by lying in Shell holes where they remained until dark about 30yds in front of their original line. No 9 Platoon C Coy under 2nd Lieut Harrison reached X.4.d.15.1. where they were attacked by Bombers, Lieut Harrison being killed but Sergt Hughes carried on the attack for about 45 minutes until enfilade M.G. fire forced him to retire very heavy M.G. fire was now turned on all the attacking force, one of our M.G's. on left flank knocked out an enemy's gun. C. Coy under the barrage of our fire got about 100yds before M.G fire	

Army Form C. 2118

WAR DIARY
or
INTELLIGENCE SUMMARY
(Erase heading not required.)

12th Durham L.I.

Place	Date	Hour	Summary of Events and Information	Remarks and references to Appendices
Trenches	17/7/16		commenced, their fight was on a road running N. & S. though X.10.b. machine gun fire was by this time intense & the advance was made only by crawling. Relay made another 100 yards but was completely held up by Cross M.G. fire. at this point Commanding the Coy was killed, the left of C. Coy got to within 40 yards of German trench where a bombing fight was carried on. The enemy were reinforced by mad about 30 men who came forward in batches of 3 men for about 3/4 of an hour the company held on in trench at X.4.D.4.L but in the end were compelled to retire. The enemy's wire at this point was about 20 yds without much trace appearance. A. Coy: on left of attack had all their officers killed or wounded, the Coy covered about 70 yds before M.G. fire opened, the attackers advanced at the double & the left flank succeeded in reaching the German parapet but the R. flank was quite held up by wire Entanglements & Cross M.G. fire & progress was impossible Always at dark withdraw to their original lines bringing in all wounded The estimate of M.G's in the function of line attacked was at least 10 this many estimated at least 15. The Batt: except B. Coy was relieved by the 13th D.L.I. & returned to Tara Trench about midnight 17/18th	C.C.

Army Form C. 2118

WAR DIARY
or
INTELLIGENCE SUMMARY
(Erase heading not required.)

12th Durham L.I.

Place	Date	Hour	Summary of Events and Information	Remarks and references to Appendices
Tara Trench	19/7/16		Casualties. Officers killed - Capt. C.W. Wetenhorne - Capt. R.C. Woodhead - 2nd Lt D. Lieut. T.W. Hetherington - 2nd Lieut F. Harrison - 2nd Lieut R. Pearce-Browne. 2nd Lieut Warren. Officers wounded - Capt S. Holmes, Lieut E.W. Lafone - 2nd Lieut Francis 2nd Lieut Casson. O.R. Killed 27 O.R. Wounded 82. Missing 16. Shellshock 4.	C.E.C.
Tara Trench	18/7/16		The following message was sent by Brig. Gen. H. Page Croft on the return to Tara Trench to the Battn. "I am of opinion that the 12th D.L.I which has already done such fine work in the recent attacks did all that was possible, most of the men held on in "no mans land" for upwards of 50 minutes under a machine gun fire which was impassable. I am satisfied that not only they did their best but that their best was most gallant. The foll: was also rec'd from Gen: Williams 34th Division I consider the 12th D.L.I attacked most gallantly & did all that Soldiers could have done under the circumstances	C.E.C.

Army Form C. 2118

WAR DIARY
or
INTELLIGENCE SUMMARY
(Erase heading not required.)

12th Durham L.I.

Instructions regarding War Diaries and Intelligence Summaries are contained in F. S. Regs., Part II. and the Staff Manual respectively. Title Pages will be prepared in manuscript.

Place	Date	Hour	Summary of Events and Information	Remarks and references to Appendices
Tara Trench	16/7/16		The Battⁿ rested the whole of the day. Word came that B. Coy would be relieved during the night.	C.E.C.
Tara Trench	19/7/16		B Coy retd to Tara Trench at 5.30.a.m. having been without rations or water for 48 hours. About 6 p.m orders came for Guides to meet 1st, 2nd & 3rd ANZAC Battⁿs These Battⁿs arrived about 8 p.m & 8.30 p.m. Guides took the Battⁿs to Brigade H.Qrs in Sausage Valley & at 11 p.m the Battⁿ recⁿ orders to move to Albert. The billeting party having gone in advance. Albert shelled during late evening & night.	C.E.C.
Albert	20/7/16		Battⁿ moved at 11 a.m by Coys to FRANVILLERS arrived about 2.30 p.m. Troops all in Billets. 2nd Lieut Marks & 2nd Lieut Boyd Smith joined Battⁿ also Draft of 24 men	C.E.C. 985 f
Franvillers	21/7/16		Battⁿ rested & Bathed & recᵈ change of clothing.	C.E.C.
Franvillers	22/7/16		Battⁿ resting. Brig. Genl. Page. Croft met officers & discussed recent operations. order recᵈ to move at 1 hours notice at midnight.	C.E.C.
"	23/7/16		Church Parade for various denominations. The order for Battⁿ to be ready to move at 1 hours notice was cancelled	C.E.C.

Army Form C. 2118

12th Durham L. Infantry

WAR DIARY
or
INTELLIGENCE SUMMARY
(Erase heading not required.)

Instructions regarding War Diaries and Intelligence Summaries are contained in F.S. Regs., Part II. and the Staff Manual respectively. Title Pages will be prepared in manuscript.

Place	Date	Hour	Summary of Events and Information	Remarks and references to Appendices
Franvillers	24/7/16		Battn prepared for inspection, all Coys inspected by O/c Coys.	C.E.C
"	25/7/16		Battn inspected by 3rd Corps Commander, at 11.a.m. who after inspection spoke to whole 68th Brigade congratulating them on the work & fighting recently done. Orders recd for Batts to move to-morrow. 2nd Lieut H. Heyner took over Command of C. Coy.	C.E.C
"	26/7/16		Battn moved 8.30 a.m. & marched at 11.30 am halted close to Albert where Battn rested until 3.30 p.m. & then moved by Coys through Becourt & took over Scott's Redoubt from 1st Gloucester Regt 1st Div. weather hot & quiet time.	C.E.C
Scott's Redoubt	27/7/16		Battn spent day at Scott's Redoubt & cleared up & deepened trenches where required & at 6 p.m. moved to Contalmaison relieving 13th D.L.I. 2nd Lieuts Hughes & Sharp joined Batts at Transport	C.E.C
Contalmaison	28/7/16		Germans shelled village about 8.30–10.30 am & at odd times during the day 11th West Yorks relieved Batts about 5.30 p.m. & Batts moved to Becourt Wood end of Sausage Valley. Heavy shelling on both sides, a number of shells fell into & close to Camping Ground. Between 11 & midnight 7 new officers arrived & report to Battn in Sausage Valley viz Capt. G.A. Nicks, 2nd Lieuts L.J. Powell-Smith A.B. Wallis, C.Vaux. W.H. Lockett, C.Armstrong, J. Bottom.	C.E.C
			Casualties in Contalmaison O.R. 2 wounded " " Sausage Valley O.R. 1. Killed 1. wounded } Officers nil	

986f

WAR DIARY or **INTELLIGENCE SUMMARY**
(Erase heading not required.)

Army Form C. 2118

12th Durham L.I.

Place	Date	Hour	Summary of Events and Information	Remarks and references to Appendices
Sausage Valley	29/7/16		Battⁿ resting all day exceedingly hot. at intervals odd shells came near. 2nd Lieut A.T. Carr West rejoined Battⁿ from Picquigny, where he had acted as Town Major. Working party of 200 men carried Bombs from Contalmaison to our front line remainder of Battⁿ bathed.	C.E.C.
Sausage Valley	30/7/16		During morning Battⁿ ground was shelled. 1 Officer wounded 2nd Lieut Heppel. 1. O.R. Killed + 5 wounded. The Brigadier advised the Battⁿ to move further back + 7.p.m Battⁿ moved to E.4.A.105 + bivouaced. The following working parties were furnished. 1 Officer + 20 men to improve Bombstore at front line, also 2 guides to 11th N.F's. Remainder of Battⁿ bathed.	C.E.C.
Becourt Road	31st/7/16		Battⁿ rested + bathed + supplied 200 men for working parties. N3 100 for Carrying Sandbags to Dump at front line + 100 for carrying Grenades. Both parties were shelled + Casualties 3 O.R. Shell Shock	C.E.C.

C.E. Cummins
Major
for O/c 12th Durham L.I.

23rd Division.

68th Brigade.

1/12th BATTALION

DURHAM LIGHT INFANTRY

AUGUST 1 9 1 6

Army Form C. 2118

WAR DIARY or INTELLIGENCE SUMMARY

(Erase heading not required.)

12th Durham L.I. Vol II

Place	Date	Hour	Summary of Events and Information	Remarks and references to Appendices
Becourt Road	1/8/16		Orders rec'd for Batt" to move at 3 p.m to Shelter Wood. 200 men supplied for Carrying Party.	CEC
Shelter Wood	2/8/16		Batt" moved 3 p.m arrive Shelter Wood & bi'c'd over about 5.30pm. Batt" supplied 200 men for working Party during morning. Batt" moved to Front Line at 5 p.m & relieved 11th Sherwood Foresters in Front Line A & B Pozieres	CEC
Front Line	3/8/16		Heavy shelling by Germans on Front line. Batt" did certain work on the trenches. Our Snipers were very successful & Patrols & bombing parties did considerable work.	CEC
"	4/8/16		Line again shelled, usual work carried out, snipers & bombers again successful.	CEC
O.G. Line No. 2.	5/8/16		Batt" moved during day to O.G. Line No 1 & were relieved by 11th N.F. This line was shelled by Enemy during day & night. Ration parties provided for Batt" in Front Line	CEC
O.G. 2	6/8/16		Considerable enemy activity during day. Batt" improved Line & supplied ration & water parties.	CEC
O.G. No. 2	7/8/16		Batt" relieved about 5 p.m by 12th H.L.I & Batt" ret'd to Becourt Road about 8 p.m.	CEC

Army Form C. 2118

WAR DIARY
or
INTELLIGENCE SUMMARY
(Erase heading not required.)

12th Durham L.I.

989f

Place	Date	Hour	Summary of Events and Information	Remarks and references to Appendices
Becourt Road	8/8/16		Battⁿ relieved at 5 am by 9th Black Watch. Battⁿ moved 6.15 am to La Houssaye & arrived about 1.15 pm.	C.O.C.
La Houssaye	9/8/16		Battⁿ rested all day, time cleaning kit etc	C.O.C.
La Houssaye	10/8/16		Battⁿ rested all day - Kit inspection & Physical Drill in morning. Transport left 3 pm with all Baggage	C.O.C.
La Houssaye	11/8/16		Battⁿ moved at 10 am for Frechencourt & entrained at 5 pm. arrived Longpré at 10.30 pm. marched to Engine arriving 1 am of 12th.	C.O.C.
Engine	12/8/16		Remained Engine until 11.30 pm & marched to Longpre to Entrain.	C.O.C.
Eecke	13/8/16		Entrained at 2 am & left about 3 am arrived Bailleul about 1 pm marched to Eecke arriving 5.30 pm men in Farms.	C.O.C.
Eecke	14/8/16		Battⁿ rested.	C.O.C.
Eecke	15/8/16		Battⁿ moved by road at 2.30 pm to area near Steenwerck & arrived about 6 pm & billeted in various farms.	C.O.C.

Army Form C. 2118.

WAR DIARY
or
INTELLIGENCE SUMMARY
(Erase heading not required.)

Instructions regarding War Diaries and Intelligence Summaries are contained in F. S. Regs., Part II. and the Staff Manual respectively. Title Pages will be prepared in manuscript.

9907

Place	Date	Hour	Summary of Events and Information	Remarks and references to Appendices
Steenwerck Area	16/6/16		Battⁿ cleaned equipment etc. All new officers lectured on Trench work.	CEC
"	17/6/16		Battⁿ moved 7.30pm for Armentières arrived 10pm, whole Battⁿ in Billet. Draft of 80 men arrived at Steenwerck & joined Battⁿ.	CEC
Armentières	18/6/16		½ Battⁿ drilled near Pont Nieppe for 4 hours, working party of 200 men at 8.45pm.	CEC
"	19/6/16		A regular daily working party of 25 men for R.E. loading sent during our stay in this position. Brig. Genⁿ Page Croft met all officers & congratulated Battⁿ for work done whilst the comm'd Brigade. Party of officers visited front line trenches – working parties supplied 200 men at night	CEC
	20/6/16		Church parade – for Battⁿ also R.C.s & other denominations. 100 men supplied for working party.	CEC
	21/6/16		Working parties supplied as follows 100 men morning + 200 evening these parties were detailed for each day during stay in Armentières	CEC
	22/6/16		Officers not on working parties visited front line trenches - working parties as on 21ˢᵗ.	CEC
	23/6/16		Officers visited front line – working parties as on 21ˢᵗ	CEC

Army Form C. 2118

WAR DIARY
or
INTELLIGENCE SUMMARY
(Erase heading not required.)

12th Durham L.I.

Place	Date	Hour	Summary of Events and Information	Remarks and references to Appendices
Armentieres	24/8/16		A. & B. Coy moved to Le Bizet relieved 11th N.F. owing to line being extended. Working parties as before.	C.E.C.
Front Line Trenches	25/8/16		Battn moved to front line trenches no. 91-95 & relieved 13th D.L.I. at 7.30 a.m. Line very quiet all day. Brigadier Genl Colville inspected the line.	C.E.C.
"	26/8/16		Very small amount of shelling by enemy few T. Mortars, we replied. Work continued on front line. 1 Coy of 13th D.L.I at Stobeum Redoubt furnished carrying parts for front line.	C.E.C.
"	27/8/16		Nothing to report. 2 Casualties. Good deal of Aircraft activity principally ours.	C.E.C.
"	28/8/16		Front line quiet except for T. Mortars. – 2 Officers visited & attended the demonstration of attack by Stokes Mortars & T.Ms at Brogues	C.E.C.
"	29/8/16		Nothing to report except the Gas attack postponed owing to change of wind.	C.E.C.
"	30/8/16		Very dull weather – nothing to report from front line	C.E.C.

Army Form C. 2118

WAR DIARY
or
INTELLIGENCE SUMMARY
(Erase heading not required.)

12th Durham L.I.

Place	Date	Hour	Summary of Events and Information	Remarks and references to Appendices
Front Line Trenches 91/95	31/8/16	1.30 a.m.	Gas discharged from left of left Coy. T.98. Very slight German shelling by Artillery but considerable by Trench Mortars. M.G. fire steady the whole time, it commenced about 2-3 minutes after gas discharged. Fire kept up for about 2-3 hours. Casualties 3 Killed - 6 wounded.	C.S.C.

C E Cumming Major
for Lt Colonel
Comdt 12th Durham L.I.

1/9/16

WAR DIARY or INTELLIGENCE SUMMARY

Army Form C. 2118

vol 12 8/7 12th Durham L.I.

Place	Date	Hour	Summary of Events and Information	Remarks and references to Appendices
Front Line 91-96	1/9/16		Enemy more active - our T.M's retaliated also R.Grenades. Considerable Sniping over Side, our Snipers reduced number of Enemy Snipers, much less from them. Arrangements for Relief cancelled. Casualties O.R. 1 killed - 2 wounded	CCC
"	2nd/9/16		Party of Officers from 9th Royal Scots came up to look over line - much quieter than yesterday. Gas alarm given by 69th Brigade afterwards cancelled.	CCC
"	3rd/9/16		Batt's relief Commenced 2.30pm & Completed by 4.45pm. 9th Rye Scots taking over our line. Batt" marched to Camp Nr Bailleul arrived about 7.30pm.	CCC
Nr Metteren	4/9/16		Batt" moved 10.30 am to billets at X.5.C. Nr Metteren arriving about 12.30pm. Divisional General inspected Batt" on route.	CCC
"	5/9/16		Batt" moved 11.30 am for Bailleul Station entrained at 1.30pm for St Omer. Batt" detrained there marched to Ouest Mont K.26.27 & were billeted there arriving about 6.30pm. Transport moved with A.S.C. Coy. billeted at Staples.	CCC SB+ JB
Ouest Mont	6/2/16		Batt" drilled morning & afternoon. Inspected by C.O. at 5.30pm. Transport arrived 2pm.	CCC

WAR DIARY
or
INTELLIGENCE SUMMARY
(Erase heading not required.)

Army Form C. 2118

12th Durham L.I.

Place	Date	Hour	Summary of Events and Information	Remarks and references to Appendices
Ouest Mont	7/9/16		Battⁿ inspected at 9.30 p.m. by Brigadier Gen. Cabrille D.S.O. & later the Divisional General was also present. Bathing for Battⁿ in afternoon. Major Moore G.S.O No 2 visited Battⁿ & lectured to Junr Officers & all N.C.O's of Battⁿ at 3 p.m.	CRC
"	8/9/16		All Coys drilled morning - Battⁿ sports held in afternoon.	CRC
"	9/9/16		Coys. drilled morning & in afternoon completion of Battⁿ sports. C.O. presented prizes.	CRC
"	10/9/16		Battⁿ moved at 9.45 a.m. to entrain at Andruick for Longeau in Amiens arrived 9 p.m. & moved at 9.45 p.m. for Moulin-aux-Bois.	CRC
Moulin aux-Bois	11/9/16		Arrived about 2.30 a.m. Battⁿ in Billets & Bivouac. Battⁿ rested during day	CRC
Millencourt	12/9/16		Battⁿ marched to Millencourt at 8.30 am arrived 1.15 p.m. Battⁿ in Billets	CRC
"	13/9/16		Battⁿ drilled in morning & new bombers & snipers recd special instruction	CRC
"	14/9/16		Battⁿ drilled. N.C.O's & Officers recd special instruction in consolidation of trenches & wiring etc. This was afterwards given to the men by Lectures. Inspection of kits by C.O.	CRC

Army Form C. 2118

WAR DIARY
or
INTELLIGENCE SUMMARY
(Erase heading not required.)

12th Durham L.J

Instructions regarding War Diaries and Intelligence Summaries are contained in F. S. Regs., Part II. and the Staff Manual respectively. Title Pages will be prepared in manuscript.

Place	Date	Hour	Summary of Events and Information	Remarks and references to Appendices
Millencourt	15/9/16		Batt" at 6.30 am awaiting orders to move at 10 minutes notice all kits ready & at 11.30 Batt" moved to Becourt wood by Coy's. Trans Batt" arrived about 2 pm & are bivouacked	CBC
Becourt Wood	16/9/16		Batt" still in Becourt Wood. Men did Physical Exercises etc	CBC
"	17/9/16		At Becourt Wood - Church parade 11 a.m.	CBC
"	18/9/16		Batt" moved 12.30 pm - to take over line Gourlay Trench relieved 11th Argyle & Sutherland H. in front of Contalmaison Villa. 8 officers rel.d to Albert	CBC
Gourlay Trench	19/9/16		Transport left Becourt wood for Albert. Batt" still at Gourlay Trench	CBC
"	20/9/16		Batt" still in support. Casualties 1. O.R. wounded 2nd Lieut G.P.F Thomas joined Batt"	CBC
"	21/9/16		Party of Officers went forward to look over front line trenches at Martinpuich Carrying party supplied 1. N.C.O & 20 men for Carrying Stokes Mortar Amm. from Contalmaison Dump to front line Batt" Lines shelled Casualties Officers 1 killed 2nd Lieut Armstrong wounded Capt" Heyner & Price O.R. 7 kil	CBC

1875 Wt. W593/826 1,000,000 4/15 J.B.C. & A. A.D.S.S./Forms/C. 2118.

Army Form C. 2118

WAR DIARY or INTELLIGENCE SUMMARY
(Erase heading not required.)

12th Durham L. I.

Place	Date	Hour	Summary of Events and Information	Remarks and references to Appendices
Gourlay Trench	22/9/16		Batt.s were photographed by War Office photographer. at 7.15 p.m moved to Front line & relieved 11th West Yorks. left of Batt" on Bapaume Road + R. on Pine Trench Casualties Officers nil. O.R. 3 Killed - 10 wounded, all casualties took place at Gun Pit Road. During the relief, heavy barrage was put over by enemy. This caused delay in relief which was not completed until 10 p.m.	CEC
Front line	23/9/16		Batt.s lines heavily shelled during day - a patrol 1 Officer & 2 men went forward to find out if T 26th avenue was held. Information brought in that it was strongly held - the patrol left at 7.30 p.m & ret.d about 11 p.m Casualties O.R. 3 killed 6 wounded	CEC.
"	24/9/16		Orders rec.d 12 midnight 23/24 for Batt.s to attack T. 26th Avenue. 2 Platoons were detailed & in addition Bombers. They left trenches at 5 am but were unable to make much progress owing to heavy M.G. fire from 2 points "13.2.9 & 5.3 & "17. These points had not been secured also information was rec.d that all were silenced The attacking force were caught between cross M.G. fire from these points + were after some time compelled to return to their original trenches Casualties 1. Officer 2nd Lieut Bottom + 5.O.R. Killed – 27 O.R wounded.– 1 O.R. Shell Shock	CEC.
"	25/9/16		Batt.s were relieved about 5. am + ret.d to D.G.1. but owing to heavy losses sustained by 10th N.F. 2 Coys were ordered to return to Front line + at 7.15 p.m remaining 2 Coys went forward to Front line. Heavy Shelling all day Casualties 1 O.R killed 3. O.R wounded	CEC

WAR DIARY or INTELLIGENCE SUMMARY
(Erase heading not required.)

Army Form C. 2118

12th Durham L.I.

Place	Date	Hour	Summary of Events and Information	Remarks and references to Appendices
Front Line	26/9/16		Shelling by enemy not so heavy, but 26th Avenue heavily shelled by our artillery. Enemy retaliated on Martinpuich - Factory & Gun Pit Lanes. 7.30 p.m. Patrol of 1 Officer & 2 men went out to reconnoitre 26th Avenue, whilst patrol was out Batt'n relieved by 8th K.O.Y.L.I. & Batt'n moved in small parties to The Dingle on FRICOURT- Contalmaison Road. Patrol ret'd about 11 p.m. reported 26th Avenue unoccupied but strong points 2.9 & 5.3 were held as Very lights were constantly fired from there. Batt'n arrived at Billet about 12 midnight. Casualties 3 O.R. killed - 25 wounded. 1 Officer wounded. 2 Shell Shock	CEC
The Dingle	27/9/16		Batt'n resting.	CEC
"	28/9/16		Transport moved from Albert to Chapes Spur Becourt Wood - Batt'n supplied working party 3 Officers & 100 men for cleaning & rep'g roads 'round Contalmaison.	CEC
"	29/9/16		2nd Lieut W. M. Blenkinsop joined Batt'n. Working party supplied 100 men for unloading R.E. Stores at Contalmaison.	CEC
"	30/9/16		Working party of 50 men supplied to dig assembly Trench E. of Martinpuich, also 50 men working in relief with 11th NF's carrying grenades etc. from Pella Dump to H.Q. Dump Martinpuich. Casualties 4. O.R. wounded.	CEC

C. E. Cummins Major
for O/C 12th Durham L.I.

WAR DIARY or INTELLIGENCE SUMMARY

Army Form C. 2118

12th Durham L.I. Vol 13

Place	Date	Hour	Summary of Events and Information	Remarks and references to Appendices
The Dingle	1916 Oct 1		Working Parties supplied 50 men carrying Stores & 50 men on Water Parties. The time has now been put back 1 hour - Batt's under orders to move at ½ hours notice - all prepared.	
"	2/10/16		Working Parties as before viz 50 men carrying Stores & 50 on Water duty. Orders rec'd 11 a.m. for Batt's to move to Gourlay Trench, very wet. "Batt" moved at 4.30 p.m. to Gourlay Trench & were all established about 6.30 p.m.	
Gourlay Trench	3/10/16		The Battalion moved to Hook & Eye Trench at 8.30 p.m. - At 12 now moved to CRESCENT ALLEY relieving the 5th N.F. - B Co in BLAYDON TRENCH were heavily shelled - also the entrance to CRESCENT ALLEY constantly shelled.	
Crescent Alley	4/10/16		Battalion in CRESCENT ALLEY. Heavy shelling all day. Supplies party of 100 men to carry Bombs for railway to the Bomb dump.	
"	5/10/16		Battalion in CRESCENT ALLEY. Heavy shelling	

Army Form C. 2118

WAR DIARY or INTELLIGENCE SUMMARY

12th DURHAM L.I.

9954

Place	Date	Hour	Summary of Events and Information	Remarks and references to Appendices
CRESCENT ALLEY	6/10/16	—	Battalion in CRESCENT ALLEY. — Relieved the 11th N.F. in O.G. 1 & 2 about 8 p.m. Evening quiet.	
O.G. 1 & 2	7/10/16	—	Battalion in O.G. 1 & 2. At 1.45 p.m. the Battalion attacked the SUNKEN ROAD — SE of LE SARS. At 1.0 p.m. he first 118 Rockets o/c C Coy took his Coy forward and occupied the TRENCHES. At 1.45 p.m. A Co. & C Co. attached with D & B Co. in Support owing to heavy M.G. fire A Co. were held up. Meanwhile C Coy arrived with 2 platoons of D Coy under 2/Lt. A.T. Hunt reached SUNKEN RD. They were then supported by the remaining 2 platoons of D Coy under 2/Lt. W.L. Hughes who consolidated the position & assisted in repelling several counter attacks on the enemy who went attempting to recoup over the ridge beyond (Butte of W[arlencourt]) thus came up & advanced about 450 yds beyond SUNKEN RD. & continued. They ended up with SUNKEN RD by a chain of S.P. Points. Our position was twenty killed by the enemy throughout the night. Casualties, Officers: Killed 2/Lt W.H. Lockett. Wounded — 2/Lt W.H. Lowes, A.T. Hunt, A.E. Hales, Wallace, Hypall, Legatt; Missing — 2/Lt Telfer. NCOs & men: Killed 31, Wounded — 86. We took about 70 prisoners. Heavily shelled. Relieved by 8/10th GORDONS. Batt. moved to BECOURT WOODS.	A3
BECOURT WOODS	8/10/16	—	Rested in BECOURT WOODS	A3
"	9/10/16	—	Congratulatory messages received from G.O.C. 3rd Corps; G.O.E. 23rd Div. G.O.C. 15th Div.	A3
"	11/10/16	—	Inspected & congratulated by G.O.C. 3rd Corps. Entrained at ALBERT for LONGPRÉ. At 13 coys left at 3 p.m.	A3
ERGNIES	12/10/16	—	Arrived at LONGPRÉ about 5 A.M. Marched to ERGNIE's Billets 8.15 A.M.	A3

WAR DIARY or INTELLIGENCE SUMMARY

Army Form C. 2118

(Erase heading not required.)

Place	Date 1916	Hour	Summary of Events and Information	Remarks and references to Appendices
ERGNIE	Oct 13		Left Ergnie 2 p.m. marching to Onenx. Major Cummins left for a Senior Officers' course at Aldershot. Capt. Pearce Mo appointed 2/c in command.	JHP
ONEUX	14		Morning spent in cleaning equipment.	JHP
	15		At 2 a.m. marching to St Riquier when we entrained 4:30 am for Poperinghe. We are Brigade commanding 68' Bde as General Critchell has gone on in advance. Battalion detrained at Proven about 2:30 p.m. marched about 8 miles to Toronto Camp.	JHP
TORONTO CAMP POPERINGHE	16		Battalion left for Ypres about 4:30 p.m. by train. Billeted at BUND	JHP
ZILLEBEKE BUND	17		Moved up into L section L Brigade, on L being on MENIN ROAD. At the TUILERIES. A.C.A Companies in line from L to R. B C in support.	JHP
" "	18		Quiet day. A Co moved to YPRES in reserve. At the moved up to HALFWAY Ho. Transport moved to	JHP
" "	19		Quiet day in line.	JHP
" "	20		Lt. Col Machlyn to England on leave. Capt Pearce took on command. Relieved by 13' Btl. Billeted in HOSPICE YPRES.	JHP
YPRES	21		Men cleaned billets & equipment. Colonel when B Co was billeted was trained. 2 Lt Thomas started M.G. class of 8 men.	JHP
" "	22		Service by Rev J.N. Batchelor in HOSPICE. Sgt W. Welden left for cadet course prior to obtaining a commission.	JHP

1916

WAR DIARY or INTELLIGENCE SUMMARY

Army Form C. 2118

Place	Date 1916	Hour	Summary of Events and Information	Remarks and references to Appendices
YPRES	Oct 23		Entrained at YPRES about 8.30 pm for Poperinghe, where the battalion were v. comfortably billeted.	JMP
POPERINGHE	24		Issue of straw for sleeping on. Rain practically incessant.	JMP JMP
"	25		Gas demonstration. Men bore rapid ino filla.	JMP
"	26		Physical drill; rifle exercises; lectures to NCO's.	JMP
"	27		Battalion bathed in morning. Inspected by General Plumer, GOC 2d Army, who decorated Ptes Kilham & Badger DCM DSO Pte Dilson MM day. work party at YPRES at night.	JMP
"	28		Bayonet & M. Gys. men paraded to inspect new knives. dull & wet & rifts received spoiled instruction in rifle exercises.	JMP
"	29		Left Poperinghe at dusk by train for YPRES. Studied bombardment about THE BLUFF a PLOEGSTEERT 5.15 pm. Relieved 8" KOYLI & Liedn R brigade; A & R pond; B & L pond; & to support in NAPLE COPSE; C to reserve at THE BUND. 2d's Coln Bndt. Shells left to by land on huts.	JMP JMP
Trenches	30/31		Living dry grind. Front line knee deep in water in places. C.O. to hot. hgs. work parties to find all day.	JMP JMP

Willalyspor wood deferring
to Denham

Army Form C. 2118

WAR DIARY or INTELLIGENCE SUMMARY
(Erase heading not required.)

12' Durham L.I. Vol. 14

Place	Date	Hour	Summary of Events and Information	Remarks and references to Appendices
France (Boesinghe)	1916 Nov 1		Lt Col MacGregor rejoined Battalion from leave to England. Companies wired a considerable portion of their front. Rain in morning.	JHB
— do —	Nov 2		Very quiet uneventful day. A & B companies tried to effect a machine gun took Position. Relieved by 13' NF who relieved from Ypres 5 p.m. Battalion established at ZILLEBEKE BUND 9.45 p.m. C & D Companies supplied work parties at night.	JHB
BUND	Nov 3		Morning spent in cleaning trenches at BUND; who tried boats laid down. Large work parties at night. Gum Boots issued. At 12.15 p.m. one of our balloons broke away, the occupant descended in a parachute. 2/Lt Grimwade, 12' D.L.I. and 68' Bde appointed Staff Captain 70' Bde	JHB
— do —	Nov 4 & 5		At Zillebeke Bund. Large work parties nightly for carrying RE supplies & work in line. On morning of 5' General Babington inspected the Bund.	JHB
— do —	Nov 6		Relieved 13' NF at DORMY HOUSE; 10' NF on R; 65' Bde on L. So on R; Cowt front line; B in support of MAPLE COPSE; A & C in rear of BUND.	JHB
Trenches	Nov 7		Enemy very quiet. Moonlight nights prevented wiring operations CROSS ST & VIGO were carried & repaired; firesteps & ornaments in front line. Trench boats laid from MAPLE COPSE to SANCTUARY WOOD. On night 8/9 considerable artillery activity.	JHB
— do —	Nov 8 & 9		about 2 divisions N of battalion. Any cars seen behind on improved of THE BUND Relieved by 8' KOYLI. Batt. proceeded to MONTREAL CAMP by train from YPRES	JHB
MONTREAL CAMP	Nov 10		being established in camp about 11 p.m.	JHB

WAR DIARY
or
INTELLIGENCE SUMMARY. 1/2 Durham L.I.
(Erase heading not required.)

Army Form C. 2118

Place	Date 1916	Hour	Summary of Events and Information	Remarks and references to Appendices
MONTREAL CAMP	Sept 11		Companies were inspected by C.O. in morning. Draft of 90 men arrived. Kit inspections by companies in afternoon.	AAF
"	" 12		Classes held in wiring, bombing & Lewis gun work. B Co. employed under R.E. in roofing huts of MONTREAL EXTENSION CAMP.	AAF
"	" 13		Company drill, bayonet fighting in morning. Drainage of camp received huts in afternoon.	AAF
"	" 14		Special training instruction under Capt ATC Asst. Party sent to help Trans- port to improve this line. Football in afternoon.	AAF
"	" 15		Special instruction the classes carried on. GOC & Corps inspects camp.	AAF
"	" 16		All & officiains made good. Inspection of Bn. by C.O. Aeroplane fight on camp; our machine forced to descend. Left camp 5 p.m. to relieve 8th Royal in Barracks, YPRES.	AAF
Barracks YPRES	" 17 " 18		Relief complete 8.30 p.m. large smoke patrols (all men = Bn.) provided daily.	AAF
"	" 19 " 20		Relieved 13" D21 in HALFWAY Ho. Relief complete 8.30 p.m. An R; Bn. & Hd. hies; C in support LEINSTER ST; D in reserve HALFWAY HOUSE.	AAF
Trenches				

WAR DIARY or INTELLIGENCE SUMMARY

Army Form C. 2118

12: Durham L.I.

Place	Date 1916	Hour	Summary of Events and Information	Remarks and references to Appendices
Trenches	Nov 21		Misty morning allowed a considerable amount of firing to be done. Very quiet.	AHA
	22		B Co. Wire party out in morning some shells. Patrols by Capt Stevens, 2nd Lt O'Brien & Capt Chambers brought back valuable information. C Co commenced bits wiring dug outs in support line.	AHA
	23		New observation post constructed by Bn observer. Wiring continued. A Co	AHA
	24		fresh some on new MG emp. Hostile artillery much active but in on R. Bde Sector. Regent St. Badly shelled; the damage. Last to be repaired before relief. Relieved by 13" DLI. Bn proceeded to Barracks YPRES being relieved at 9.30 p.m. 1 Platoon 2 Co under 2nd Lt C Vaux at Noah's Grange. Bn Cadres opened at Barracks.	AHA
Barracks YPRES				
" "	25 26 27 28		Days work periods formed nightly to work in lines & carrying R.E. stores. All men including H.Q. men adj & adjutants had to take later to supply these parties. Special attention was paid to inspections of feet.	AHA
" "	29		Bath parties in morning. Artillery bombardment by us on our L. Relieved by 9" Yorks. Marching off from them to MONREAL CAMP by J. Infantry in of companies by C.O. Men refilled. Parties of 80 men each in the morning.	AHA
MONREAL CAMP	30		Drawing of camp kit. [signed] Willie(?) Selbegser(?) Lt. Colonel C.O. 12' Durham L.I.	AHA

WAR DIARY or INTELLIGENCE SUMMARY.
(Erase heading not required.)

Army Form C. 2118.

Vol 15 12th Durham L.I.

Place	Date	Hour	Summary of Events and Information	Remarks and references to Appendices
MONTREAL CAMP	1		Camp inspected by G.O.C. Bde in morning. Refitting mens clothing. Football held in afternoon. Sgts Mess Officers 6-5.	
	2		Musketry training. Grille in morning. Fire Picquet practised. This section all kits supplied with Fins Odeurs.	
	3		Church Parade in div cinema. Lt Col Stackhyn left for by had as a matrix head. Boys work parties supplied.	
	4		Inspection of camp by G.O.C. Bde. Bug Column reported fortnightly on own cookers & cooking. Work parties at night.	
	4½		Instruction in guard mounting. Stations, also Lectures.	
	5		Rain prevented work. Officers football match of 13th – drawn 1-1. Stayed in Montreal Camp. Sug W.H.E. work could be done as the men were not made late every night.	
	7		Left camp 2.45, had bad planning up to Vlamertinghe. Relieved 8th Royal at DORNY. MD.	
Trenches DORNY M.D.	8		Wonderful turn in trenches. Every opportunity taken to work but full moon made sniping difficult. Cleaned trench & filled back supplies in sacks.	
	9			
	10		New day all work in NAPLES COPSE. On all things started on our trenches at midday. 8"	

WAR DIARY
or
INTELLIGENCE SUMMARY

Army Form C. 2118.

Place	Date	Hour	Summary of Events and Information	Remarks and references to Appendices
Trenches DOR'N'Y Ho	Dec 10		Capt Wotsell Roome left for a Sanitary Course at Steynbrick. Lt Bramwell Bazron's Returned. Relieved by 13" M.I. proceeding to HOSPICE, YPRES. About 7 p.m. or thereabouts in the Bluff sector - considerable mortar activity as a result. Major R. T. Joudell, 13th M.I. joined the battalion.	JMP
	11			JMP
YPRES HOSPICE	12			JMP
	13		Men out on work parties nightly. Latrines & cleaning up in day-time.	JMP
	14			
	15		Steady bombardment at times about 7 a.m. R. sector of R. brigade, supports & 2 YPRES heavily shelled 4 p.m. N.E. we raided 4.15 p.m. Relief cancelled.	JMP
	16		left HOSPICE 5 p.m. to relieve 13th M.I. at DORNY HO. An R.E. Cpl & Cpl C.O. in front of NAPLE C. N.T.O. is supposed RIBDAN or... 1 man killed & 2 during relief.	JMP
Trenches DORNY Ho	17		Hand trench machine gun 19" but there a camouflaged new Hill 60. Machine fellows.	JMP
	18			
	19			
	20		In morning enemy ran the brigade front was heavily shelled. CRAB CRAWL blocked. Enemy a Artillery start shooting at YPRES 13" M.I. 2 men (A + C Co) wounded.	JMP

WAR DIARY
or
INTELLIGENCE SUMMARY.
(Erase heading not required.)

Army Form C. 2118.

Instructions regarding War Diaries and Intelligence Summaries are contained in F. S. Regs., Part II. and the Staff Manual respectively. Title pages will be prepared in manuscript.

Place	Date	Hour	Summary of Events and Information	Remarks and references to Appendices
THE BUND	Dec 20		relieved in at 8.45 p.m. ATS B Co proceeded to THE BUND. C Co attached to R. batt in NAPLE C.M.	HP
	21		Both parties supplied from THE BUND. 6 p.m. on 22 or forward army lines about HL	HP
	22		BLUFF Section. Enemy relatively active on ZILLEBEKE St.	HP
	23		Relieved by 9' YORKS, 8.45 p.m. Left YPRES siding 12.30, arriving camp 2.15.	HP
MONTREAL CAMP	24		Both parties supplied 7.30 a.m. & at night. B Co. at disposal of O.C. B Co	HP
	25		Band of 8' Regt. plays carols 7 a.m. Voluntary service 9.30 am. His Xmas dinner 1 p.m. — Pork, but plum pudding, fruit, beer etc. Free entrance to Cinema at night. Lights out 7 p.m. No work parties.	HP
	26		Officers 13: ER1 bed 12: officers 3-2. Small work party. A Co at disposal or A Co.	HP
	27		Both parties sack afternoon. Rifleing OC Co. to allnam A C Co to HL 27:	HP
	28		Created a training camp opposite Orderly Room.	HP
	29		Transport inspected by GOC 68: Bde. Favorable report followed. Bde. Cy. of. own team 4/13: ER1	HP
	30		Coming Parade. Maj. Tyndell to hospital at Palaise. Capt. Sellrane on leave; left Havrin as Lowvan. Brig. Boxing tournament in afternoon. Bought of Cinema receipts 166 frances.	HP
	31		Left camp 3-45 to relieve 8' Regt at HALF WAY HO. Relief complete 8.30 p.m. A Co reach. B Co. HEINSBE ST M: C Co. R. Parti. D Co L Parti. HO at Railway Cutting.	HP

[signed] Lunday 12: DLI

WAR DIARY or INTELLIGENCE SUMMARY.

Army Form C. 2118.

(Erase heading not required.)

12' Batt. The Durham L.I.

Place	Date	Hour	Summary of Events and Information	Remarks and references to Appendices
TRENCHES.	1/7		Battalion in trenches. "D" Coy at BIRR CROSS ROADS and the CULVERT. "A" Coy ZOUAVE WOOD. "B" Coy ROSSLYN ST in Support and "C" Coy in reserve at HALF WAY HOUSE. Battalion HQ at Cutting near HELL FIRE CORNER. Enemy Trench Mortar Shelled during the morning. About 4.0 pm the CULVERT Post was heavily shelled for about half an hour. Two Sergts and one Sketcher known Killed. No men known acc - otherwise a very quiet day.	
"	2/7		Battalion in trenches - nothing unusual to report.	
"	3/7		Trenches. Half way house and Birr Cross Road Slightly shelled. Colonel MacGregor returned from one months leave.	
"	4/7		Very quiet day. Relieved in the evening by 13th Bn Durham Light Infantry. The Battalion moving to Infantry Barracks. Ypres in DRainier.	
Infantry Barracks	5-7/7		Battalion in Infantry Barracks. Whole working parties provides - practically the Whole Battalion being out working.	
	8/7		Battalion relieved the 13' Durham Light Infantry - relief	

WAR DIARY
or
INTELLIGENCE SUMMARY.
(Erase heading not required.)

Army Form C. 2118.

2 Bn. The Durham L.I.

Place	Date	Hour	Summary of Events and Information	Remarks and references to Appendices
(contd.)	8/7		Complete at 8.30 p.m. Ypres and vicinity were heavily shelled during the day. The enemy obtaining one direct hit on the footbridge over the MOAT.	(2)
TRENCHES	9/7		Battalion in trenches. B Coy at BIRR CROSS ROADS and THE CULVERT. A Coy ZOUAVE WOOD. "C" Coy ROSSLYN STREET D60 at HALFWAY HOUSE. Battalion HQrs at HALFWAY HOUSE. The day was very quiet on our front although a large number of heavy shells were going in the direction of YPRES.	
	10/7		Battalion in trenches - exceptionally quiet day.	(3)
	11/7		Battalion in trenches - a good deal of aeroplane activity - German Howze shelled as usual	(3)
	12/7		Trenches. The support trs & reserve trenches of the Division on our left was heavily shelled about 3.30 p.m. The Battalion was relieved in the evening by the 13 D.L.I. We	(4)
	13/7		proceeded to INFANTRY BARRACKS in DPERLIN. Battalion in Divisional Reserve at the INFANTRY BARRACKS. Manual	(5)

WAR DIARY
or
INTELLIGENCE SUMMARY.
(Erase heading not required.)

Army Form C. 2118.

12Bn The Durham Light Infantry

Place	Date	Hour	Summary of Events and Information	Remarks and references to Appendices
(cont.)	13/7/17		O.C. Looking Parties Strides. Colonel W.D. MacGregor proceeds on a commanding Officers Course.	D.
Infantry Bks.	14/7/17		Work parties strides for R.E.	D.
"	15/7/17		Work parties strides. Battalion Baths in the Infantry Barracks	D.
"	16/7/17		Have Battalion has relieved by the 19th West Yorks Riding Regt. The Battalion has relieved by the 19th West Yorks Riding Regt. We entrained at YPRES & detrained at VLAMTINGHE. arriving at MONTREAL CAMP at 9-30 p.m. Work party of 50.0R attached RE for laying pipes.	D.
Montreal Camp.	17/7/17		Heavy fall of Suns. Rifts. Lecture on Censorship at Cinema	D.
"	18/7/17		WINNIPEG CAMP at 2.0 pm 12 Off & 4 NCO's per Coy attend Lecture on of Suns. & a very keen frost. Kit Inspection in huts and a short run. Lecture on Barrage at Cinema at POPERINGHE at 2 pm.	D.
"	19/7/17		Drill & physical exercises. Instead in the afternoon 100 OR proceed to work party at YPRES. 25 men bathing at VLAMHINTINGHE with Corps Armoury Coy. Lecture at Cinema WINNIPEG CAMP at 2.0 pm on Dugouts.	D.
"	20/7/17		Drill & Bathing. Colonel recipient went to G.H.Q. 3rd Line to meet Brigadier. They reminisces he took his persons to a practice	D.

WAR DIARY
or
INTELLIGENCE SUMMARY.
(Erase heading not required.)

Army Form C. 2118.

12th Durham Light Infantry

Place	Date	Hour	Summary of Events and Information	Remarks and references to Appendices
(Contd)	20/7		About the following day.	(R)
Montreal Camp.	21/7		Battalion paraded at 9-30 pm for practice attack on CMR Trenches. The object of this attack was to practice Cooperation between RFC & the Infantry. Signalling lamps + ground sheets were used - also flares were lit in the trenches when it had been Consolidated. The Battalion marched back to Camp at 12 noon.	
"	22/7		Drill etc in the morning - 100 bombing party from coys in the evening.	(R)
"	23/7		Lecture on the Lewis gun at 11. am in Queen WINNIPEG Capel. Adjutant attended Conference at Brigade HQ at 3 pm.	(R)
"	24/7		Battalion relieves the 9th York Lancaster Regt in A Berlin in the right Brigade area. Relief Complete at 1-0 am	(R)
"	25/7		Very quiet day. Aeroplane activity.	R
"	26/7		Battalion in the line - Artillery very active on both sides but all concentrated in trench area - presumably enemy counts battery work	(R)

Army Form C. 2118.

WAR DIARY
or
INTELLIGENCE SUMMARY.
(Erase heading not required.)

12th Durham Light Infantry

Place	Date	Hour	Summary of Events and Information	Remarks and references to Appendices
VERCHES	27/7.		Battalion in trenches. To-day being the KAISER's birthday, an commenced a bombardment of the enemy's front support line at 7 a.m. with our heavy and medium trench mortars, lasting for two hours. Enemy retaliation was very feeble. One man slightly wounded from Back Minnie.	M.S.
"	28/7		Day very quiet. ZILLEBEKE heavily shelled about 3.0 p.m. The Battalion was relieved by 13th Durham Light Infantry in the evening, relief complete at 8.0 p.m. The Battalion went back to 'B' position, being in the following position. A Co. The Hospice YPRES. B Co. KRUISSTRAAT. C Co. THE BUND. D Co. CAV BARRACKS YPRES. Battalion H.Q. THE BUND.	P.S.
	29/7 30/7 31/7		Battalion in Buns — working parties provided all day.	M.

W.W. Machrays Lt. Colonel
C. O. 12 Durham L.I.

WAR DIARY
or
INTELLIGENCE SUMMARY.
(Erase heading not required.)

Army Form C. 2118.

Vol 17 /2 Bn Durham Light Infantry

Place	Date	Hour	Summary of Events and Information	Remarks and references to Appendices
TRENCHES	1/2/17		To Trenches relieving the 8th Bn Durham Light Infy. Leaving the 'Bund' at 5-30 p.m. Relief complete by 9.0 p.m.	AD
"	2/2/17		A very quiet tour. Occasional shelling of Zillebeke & trench board near MAPLE COPSE	AD
"	3/2/17			
"	4/2/17		Relieved by the 13th Bn Durham Light Infantry. Relief complete by 8.30 p.m. Battalion moves to 6 points of	
	5/2/17		The Bund - dispositions as follows. A Coy in STAFFORD ST. MAPLE COPSE. B Coy 2 platoons in STAFFORD ST & 2 platoons in WINNIPEG ST C & D Coys & Batt HQ in the Bund.	AD
To Bund				
	6/2/17		Battalion in "C" position. Usual working parties	AD
	7/2/17		found daily by the night of 7/8 about 11 pm	AD
	8/2/17		the enemy WINNIPEG ST was shelled rather heavily, the trenches being flooded but no casualties. One man wounded in MAPLE COPSE on the afternoon of the 5th	AD

Army Form C. 2118.

WAR DIARY
or
INTELLIGENCE SUMMARY.
2/5th Bn. Th. Durham Light Infantry
(Erase heading not required.)

Place	Date	Hour	Summary of Events and Information	Remarks and references to Appendices
C position	9/7/17		The Battalion were relieved by the 11th West Yorkshire Regt. Relief complete at 10-30 p.m. During the relief the enemy shelled ZILLEBEKE ⟶ & the front trench heavily & at intervals consequently the relief was held up. The Battalion marched back to	
MONTREAL CAMP	10/7/17		Battalion in MONTREAL CAMP in CORPS RESERVE. Refitting and settling down. Commanding Officer Kit Inspection. Pennies Shot Pins from 7-9.45 a.m.	M.D.
"	11/7/17		New fighting platoon Commanders organising in English to report to Han Office. Lt Colonel W.W. MacGregor proceeds to England. Major R Tyndall assumes command of the Battalion Major R Tyndall attended General Court Martial at POPERINGHE. at 10-30 a.m.	M.D.
"	12/7/17		The Commanding Officer Lt Col R Tyndall inspected his Corps and new fighting platoons in full marching order. Inter Company Football match in the afternoon.	M.D.

T2134. Wt. W708—776. 500000. 4/15. Sir J. C. & S.

Army Form C. 2118.

WAR DIARY
or
INTELLIGENCE SUMMARY. 12 Bn. Du Durham Light Infantry
(Erase heading not required.)

Place	Date	Hour	Summary of Events and Information	Remarks and references to Appendices
MONTREAL CAMP	13/2/17		Informed that the New Organised platoons need adoption	
			before resuming original Company training.	
	14/2/17		99 - O.R. arrived tostes to Companies' Draft 9	MD
"			Battalion baths at POPERINGHE. Medical Officer inspected	MD
	15/2/17		Companies on return from Baths.	
			Early morning parade - drill & training of Lewis Gunners.	MD
			Football in the afternoon.	
	16/2/17		Signalling Scheme between Regt Signallers and Aeroplanes.	
			Remainder Battalion prepared for G.O.C Brigade's Inspection Inspection	MD
			cancelled.	
	17/2/17		Battalion proceeds to trenches relieving the 8" K.O.Y.L.I in the	
			right subsector of the left Brigade Relief complete by 5.15 am	MD
			18/2/17.	
	18/2/17		Battalion in trenches. Very misty day. One man wounded	
			whilst filling sandbags in WARRINGTON AVENUE. H.Q the TUILERIES	
			two shells about 12.15 pm. A great deal of shelling down.	MD

WAR DIARY
or
INTELLIGENCE SUMMARY

(Erase heading not required.) 12 Bn The Durham L.I.

Army Form C. 2118.

Place	Date	Hour	Summary of Events and Information	Remarks and references to Appendices
TRENCHES	19/7		Battalion in trenches - weather still very Good	
			Aerial Salving done in rear of Divisional Relief.	
			D Co moving from Vince St to Maple Copse	M
	20/7		Very misty day. Great deal of Salving done. At 5 pm a heavy bombardment took place on our right preparing to a raid by the 41st Division. Consequently the enemy barrages our front and support lines. Captain D.M. Chandler Killed	
	21/7		Trenches - very quiet - misty. Work on Vince St continued	M
	22/7		Trenches Relieved by the 13th Bn Durham L.I. relief complete at 10·00 pm, the Battalion proceeding to Barracks in D positions	M M
BARRACKS YPRES	23/7 24/7 25/7		Battalion in Barracks Ypres, he movel working parties furnished to R.E.	M
	26/7		Battalion relieved by the 16th Rifle Brigade relief complete at 7·30 pm	

WAR DIARY
or
INTELLIGENCE SUMMARY. 2ⁿᵈ Bn. The Buffs L.I.

Army Form C. 2118.

Place	Date	Hour	Summary of Events and Information	Remarks and references to Appendices
	26/7/17		Coy. on relief the Battalion entrained at YPRES siding, attaining at POPERINGHE and marched to P. Camp.	
P. Camp.	27/7/17 2/8/17		Battalion in P. Camp - cleaning up generally. Battalion left P. Camp at 9.0 am, and marched to HOUTKERQUE and billets for the night. Arrived at 1.0 pm.	

Willmott
Lt Colonel
2nd Bn The Buffs L.I.

WAR DIARY
or
INTELLIGENCE SUMMARY.
(Erase heading not required.)

Vol 18 2nd Bn. The Durham Light Infantry

Army Form C. 2118.

Place	Date	Hour	Summary of Events and Information	Remarks and references to Appendices
HOUTKERQUE	1/3/17		Battalion marched off from HOUTKERQUE at 9-30 a.m. "A" Coy furnishing the advance guard and "B" Coy the rearguard. Halted for one hour at ZEGGERS-CAPPEL for dinners. Arrived at MERCKEGHEM at 3.30 p.m. Billets not good — very scattered. March discipline very good — no men fell out.	OD
MERCKEGHEM	2/3/17		Battalion in training area. Refitting and general cleaning up. Companies paraded under new organisation.	OD
"	3/3/17		Weather fine. Training — Platoon Drill, Handling Arms, Bayonet Exercises, Bomb throwing. All employs men paraded at 2.0 p.m. for 1 hours drill under 2nd in Command. Draft of 21 OR arrived — not very good. Equipment in a very bad state	OD
	4/3/17		Short run from 7-8 a.m. — 9-10 a.m. Musketry Exercises, Bayonet Exercises, Bombing, Platoon Drill, Lewis Gunners. Squatters under their Specie Officers. "A" Coy all day on Rifle range. Every man firing 10 rounds of ammunition. Draft of 23 OR arrived. Also Lieuts J.E. Rasch, H. Richardson	OD

Army Form C. 2118.

WAR DIARY
or
INTELLIGENCE SUMMARY.
(Erase heading not required.) 12th Bn The Durham Light Infantry

Instructions regarding War Diaries and Intelligence Summaries are contained in F. S. Regs., Part II. and the Staff Manual respectively. Title pages will be prepared in manuscript.

Place	Date	Hour	Summary of Events and Information	Remarks and references to Appendices
MERCKEGHEM	5/3/17		Snow fell from 6 am to 9 am. Lecture by platoon Commanders in Billets. Musketry Exercises. Bayonet Exercises and Bombing during the morning. Platoon Drill from 2-3 pm. All Employs new parades under 2nd in Command from 2-3 pm.	
"	6/3/17		"B" Company all day on Rifle Range. 7.0 - 7.45 am. Musketry Exercises. Bayonet Exercises. Bombing Exercises. Bombs under Bombing Officer. Employs new parades under 2nd in Command from 2-3 pm. The Commanding went to ST OMER to meet the Lieut General commanding XVIII Corps.	
"	7/3/17		Platoon Drill - Instruction to Junior NCOs by Second in Command and Adjutant. Brigade Signallers at work. Exercises under Platoon Commanders. "C" Coy Bombers (32) fine new Bombs moving on open tactical Line. Battalion HQ ("Fighting" & "Administrative") parades under New Organisation Scheme. Weather bitterly cold. There has been great cold. Conference of Officers of the Battalion at 6.0 pm	

Army Form C. 2118.

WAR DIARY
or
INTELLIGENCE SUMMARY. 2 Bn The Durham Light Infantry
(Erase heading not required.)

Instructions regarding War Diaries and Intelligence Summaries are contained in F. S. Regs., Part II. and the Staff Manual respectively. Title pages will be prepared in manuscript.

Place	Date	Hour	Summary of Events and Information	Remarks and references to Appendices
MERCEGHEM	8/3/17		Snow fell in the early morning. B Coy paraded under their organization at 7.15 am for Inspection by the commanding.	
			C Coy firing on Rifle Range. Platoon drill. Musketry Exercises, Bayonet Exercises & B Coy bombing throwing live bombs under Bombing Officer.	(B)
"	9/3/17		Very fine weather. Platoon drill & Platoon practice in Artillery formation in accordance with OB/1919/T GHQ. 2nd Lt M.S. O'Brien accidentally wounded.	(B) (M)(D)
"	10/3/17		Musketry Exercises, Bayonet Exercises & Bombing Exercises. Bombing Exercises, y Bayonet Exc y. Platoon practice in Artillery formation in accordance with OB/1919/T	(B)
	11/3/17		Baths from 8 am — 3 pm. Also wire musketry & Platoon Drill. In the afternoon the 1st 2nd Battalion Sports.	
	12/3/17		Usual musketry & Bayonet and bombing Exercises. Platoon attacks. Highly successful Platoon attack. A Scheme arranged for communication between	(B)

Training.

A6945 Wt. W14422/M1160 35,000 12/16 D.D. & L. Forms/C./2118/14.

WAR DIARY
INTELLIGENCE SUMMARY
(Erase heading not required.)

Army Form C. 2118.

R. Durham L.

Place	Date	Hour	Summary of Events and Information	Remarks and references to Appendices
MERCKEGHEM	12/3/17	(Col^o)	Infantry and Aeroplane were cancelled owing to wet & misty weather. Conference of Officers in the evening.	
"	13/3/17	7-7.45 A.M.	Very fine day. Musketry. Bombing & Bayonet Exercise.	M2
		9-2 P.M.	Coy Route Marches with Tactical Scheme whilst on the march.	M2
"	14/3/17	7-7.45	Musketry, Bombing & Bayonet Exercises	
		9.30-10.30	Companies practice in New Artillery Formations	
		11-12 noon		
		2-3 p.	Platoons practice in New Artillery formations in accordance with G.H.Q. O.B. 0/1919/T.	M2
"	15/3/17		Company practice in New Artillery Formations in the morning. Platoon practice in New Artillery Formations in the afternoon.	M2
"	16/3/17		Same as for 15 inst. Aeroplane Scheme cancelled owing to wet weather.	M2

WAR DIARY
or
INTELLIGENCE SUMMARY
(Erase heading not required.)

Army Form C. 2118.

2nd Dublin Regt Infy

Place	Date	Hour	Summary of Events and Information	Remarks and references to Appendices
MERCKEGHEM	17/3/19		Company Route March in full marching order	MD
"	18/3/19	7 am	Musketry, Bombing & Bayonet Exercises	
			Musketry, Bombing & Bayonet Exercises in the morning	MD
		11 am	Church Parade	
			Football match in the afternoon. Battalion teams	
			1st of 2nd Leinster Regt. Result 2 all. 1st 2CBSO.	MD
HERZEELE	19/3/19		Battalion marches to billets in HERZEELE arriving about 2.0 pm	MD
			Very hot day.	
	20/3/19		Battalion marches off at 10.15 am to 2 Camp near POPERINGHE	MD
			arriving about 12.30 pm	
	21/3/19		The C.O. and boy Commdrs went forward at 8 am to	
			reconnoitre L LINES. The Battalion left 2 camp at 12.30 pm	
			& relieves 17th R.W.F. in L. LINES. Relief complete at 9 pm	
			night of relief enemy shelled the neighbourhood of £10. no	MD
			casualties	
L LINES	22/3/19		Battalion in L LINES at the Tactical disposal of A.O.C. 115"	
			Infy Brigade. Cleaning up trenches & dugouts generally.	MD

Army Form C. 2118.

WAR DIARY
or
INTELLIGENCE SUMMARY
2 Durham Light Infantry
(Erase heading not required.)

Instructions regarding War Diaries and Intelligence Summaries are contained in F. S. Regs., Part II. and the Staff Manual respectively. Title pages will be prepared in manuscript.

Place	Date	Hour	Summary of Events and Information	Remarks and references to Appendices
L. LINES	23/7		125 men Supplies to R.E. for work on L Defences. Companies working on their own lines. Lewis Gun & Signallers classes under Specials Officers. Very quiet day.	
L. LINES	24/7		Battalion in L Lines. Usual work parties. Enemy fired about 60 rounds Battery heavily shelled.	(B)
"	25/7		Lewis machine gun Farm. Battalion in L Lines. Usual work parties.	(B)
"	26/7		Very quiet day	(B)
"	27/7		Battalion in L Line Defences. Usual work parties.	(B)
"	28/7		Provides very quiet. Enemy shelled batteries trench about Machine Gun Farm pretty heavily all day by 4 low shrapnels at intervals. Relieved by 10" M.Ls it 5 pm. Relief complete by 6-30 pm Battalion went to D camp.	(B)

Army Form C. 2118.

WAR DIARY
or
INTELLIGENCE SUMMARY. 1/2 Durhams L.I.
(Erase heading not required.)

Instructions regarding War Diaries and Intelligence Summaries are contained in F. S. Regs., Part II. and the Staff Manual respectively. Title pages will be prepared in manuscript.

Place	Date	Hour	Summary of Events and Information	Remarks and references to Appendices
D Camp A-30.C.	29/3/17		Battalion in D Camp. Bayonet fighting. Bombing. Musketry Exercises. Lewis Gunners on 100 yds Range. 250 men supplies to R.E. for work at Elverdinghe through cable	
"	30/3/17		Battalion at Baths. Cloths & Blankets sent away to be disinfected. 350 men supplies to R.E.	
"	31/3/17		Changed Dungarees clothes at the Baths. Bombing Exercises. Instruction in the use of Rifle Grenades. 350 men supplies to R.E. for working parties. Lt Colonel R Turnbull proceeds on two days leave to Calais.	

C. E. Cummins Major
Comdg 1/2 Durham L.I.

BATTALION. OPERATION. ORDERS.   (SECRET)

Reference Sheet. 28. N.W. 1/20,000.   NO. 44.

1. The Battalion will be relieved by the 10th N.F. tomorrow the 28th inst, commencing 5 P.M.
2. "A" Coy. 12th D.L.I. will be relieved by "D" Coy. 10th N.F.
   "B"   "   "   "   "   "   "   "   "   "C"   "   "   "
   "C"   "   "   "   "   "   "   "   "   "B"   "   "   "
   "D"   "   "   "   "   "   "   "   "   "A"   "   "   "
3. Platoon Guides from "A" Coy & 3 Platoons of "B" Coy from L.6. will meet incoming Battalion at B.20.b.3.7. at 5.P.M.
   Platoon Guides from "C" & "D" Coys & No.8. platoon "B" Coy will parade at Bn H.Qrs. L.8. at 4-30 P.M. They will meet the corresponding parties of the 10th N.F. at H.12.c.2.7. at 5.P.M.
4. All Defence Schemes, Trench Maps, Trench Stores etc, will be handed over.
5. All Baggage, Lewis Guns etc, must be ready for removal by 5.P.M.
6. On relief, the Battalion will withdraw to "D" Camp, A.30. Central, taking over from the 10th N.F.
7. Platoons will move independantly.
   All movement will be in parties of four, with 100 Yards distance between parties.
8. Advance parties will go forward at 9.A.M. to take over the Camp. 2nd Lt. D. Drewery will take over Bn H.Q. and & will be responsible for accomodating the Bn in Camp.
9. The Quartermaster will take over all Stores in Camp.
10. Billets must be left scrupulously clean.
11. Reliefs will be reported to Bn H.Qrs by code.

~ Acknowledge. ~

Dodd.
Capt & Adjutant
12th Bn Durham. L. Inf.

27. 3. 17.
Copy to File.
   "   " Commanding Officer
   "   " 2nd in Command
   "   " O.C. Coys.
   "   " L. Gun. Officer
   "   " T. Officer
   "   " Quartermaster
   "   " 115th INF BDE
   "   " 10th N.F.
   "   " R.S.M.

Vol / 9
Army Form C. 2118.

2' Durham Light Infy

WAR DIARY
or
INTELLIGENCE SUMMARY.
(Erase heading not required.)

Instructions regarding War Diaries and Intelligence Summaries are contained in F. S. Regs., Part II. and the Staff Manual respectively. Title pages will be prepared in manuscript.

Place	Date	Hour	Summary of Events and Information	Remarks and references to Appendices
D Camp A.30.(cont)	1/4/17		Battalion in D Camp. Chariot parade. Battalion plays 13" DLI at football in Brigade Competition. Result 12.DLI 3. 13.DLI 1. 350 men supplies to R.E.	(1)
"	2/4/17		Physical Exercises. Bombing Exercises. Musketry. Instruction in the use of Rifle Grenades. Battalion receives orders to "Stand To" to be ready to move to the training area. Officers of 12 DLI v. Officers of 13 DLI - result. 13' DLI won 4-3. 350 men supplies to R.E. for work parties. also 40 men supplies to Brigade for sundry tasks.	(2)
Strt 28 -"-	3.4.17.		Snowstorm in morning prevented parade or bgs behind, interfered SAA, gas goggles & respirators. Lecturing competition at 12.30 pm resulted in C Co winning, others clear with 2 B 2 D. In cleanliness class A Co 1st, C Co 2nd. Bath party of 250 found at 1030 to bring cats.	M
-"-	4.4.17.		Battalion moves from D Camp to NEUCKEGHEM, thence & proceeded by road with limbers— and 1 gun. Battalion entrained BRANDHOEK 1 pm detrained ESQUEL BECQ about 3 pm.	M
NEUCKEGHEM				M

WAR DIARY or INTELLIGENCE SUMMARY

Army Form C. 2118.

12th Durham L.I.

Place	Date	Hour	Summary of Events and Information	Remarks and references to Appendices
MERCKEGHEM	1917 Apr 4		Moved by road to MERCKEGHEM, according to billets 6 p.m. Transport reached billets 8.15 p.m.	AA
	Apr 5		Day spent in cleaning clothing, equipment, billets. Bn arrived BOLLEZEELE during afternoon.	AA
	6		Companies practised Trench attack or Training area in morning. Conference at night.	AA
	7		Scouting course started under 2 Lt GIBBENS. Companies practised trench attack in morning.	AA
			Officers of 12 DLI had Officers M.G.C. — 17LS at football in afternoon.	
	8		Church Parade in morning. Final of Bn. Recreation football comp: 10 NF beat 12 DLI 2-1.	AA
	9		Battalion in attack or Training area & Coy-Company comm in afternoon. 10 NF beat 12 DLI 2nd	AA
			Specialists & G.L.O. units. Bath bathes in afternoon.	
	10		Batt. battles thoroughly dry. Specialist Officers instructed the Bn as about like men in the morning.	AA
			Bath Signal competition lost by 2 Lt Dressery. 1st round of Bde Rugby Football Comp. 12 DLI v 13 DLI	
			held in arena 5 points all.	
	11		Companies on a route march 11 miles in morning. Snowstorm throughout day. His arrival	AA
			in success of Vimy Ridge.	
	12		2 Officers and 5B or left to attend to Div with Corps Commandant. Trench attack in an	AA
			junction with M.G.Cs r T.M.Bs. Replay of Rugby match in afternoon. 13 DLI beat 12 DLI. 6 tries to nil.	

Army Form C. 2118.

WAR DIARY
or
INTELLIGENCE SUMMARY.
(Erase heading not required.)

12th Durham L.I.

Instructions regarding War Diaries and Intelligence Summaries are contained in F. S. Regs., Part II. and the Staff Manual respectively. Title pages will be prepared in manuscript.

Place	Date	Hour	Summary of Events and Information	Remarks and references to Appendices
DICKEBUSCH	April 13		Practised rapid wiring of a captured position in morning.	AP
"	14		Left DICKEBUSCH 7am; arrived at ESQUELBECQ, avoided camp near BRANDHOEK, about 2 km Poperinghe. Sent forward at night to take over billets in YPRES Barracks.	AP
BRANDHOEK YPRES	15		Rained all day. 75 men ordered to Travelling Camp Reninghelst, 48 to Town Major YPRES. Left BRAND-	AP
			HOEK 4 pm for YPRES, J. 9.45. Relief of coy field 12.45 owing to congestion in barracks. Captains in barracks, H.Q. in Ramparts.	Captains
	16		280 men found for Australian Travelling party work	AP
	17		280 men working under Australian Travelling Co., 20 men cleaning Bri. Hd. Quart.	AP
	18		Same parties found as for 17. inst. Quiet day.	MP
YPRES - ZILLEBEKE	19		or Co. reconnoitred line STREET ST - WARRINGTON. Battn. relieved the 13th Durham L.I. in the Zillebeke sector. Only 500 men went into the line. 12 platoons in all & were disposed as follows. "A" Coy. 2 platoons in Vancouver St & 1 in Winnipeg St. "B" Coy 2 in Crab Crawl & 1 in Winnipeg. "C" Coy 1 in Ross St. 1 in Vancouver St & 1 in 60th Street. "D" Coy 1 - Hill St & 2 in Fort St. Relief completed about midnight.	CEC
Zillebeke	20		Work done on Wire repairing trenches, weather fine, good deal of aeroplane activity on both sides, odd shelling of rear lines & T.M. on front.	C.E.C.

Army Form C. 2118.

WAR DIARY
or
INTELLIGENCE SUMMARY.   12th Durham L.I.
(Erase heading not required.)

Instructions regarding War Diaries and Intelligence Summaries are contained in F. S. Regs., Part II. and the Staff Manual respectively. Title pages will be prepared in manuscript.

Place	Date	Hour	Summary of Events and Information	Remarks and references to Appendices
Zillebeke	21st		Weather fine, usual work continued nothing of moment took place line very quiet except for odd bursts of T.M.s. Patrols at night reported all clear.	C.E.C.
"	22nd		Weather fine, Considerable shelling of Ypres by Germans nothing on front line all going to rear lines & batteries. Line again patroled at night nothing unusual.	C.E.C.
"	23		Fine day, more shelling of Ypres & also afoot at the Tuileries & Maple Copse. We were relieved by 13th D.L.I. & Batts ret'd to Barracks Ypres about midnight. Batt's H.Qrs at Ramparts	C.E.C.
YPRES	24th		Batt's rested except for working parties, Ypres again shelled & about 20 rounds to Barracks. 3 officers visited R of our Divl front. Y3 Hill 60 sector. Jumps etc	J.C.
"	25th		Working parties; Still shelling Ypres our artillery replied very strongly. 6 officers visited the Nue 60 sector a good deal of aeroplane activity on this front.	J.C.
"	26		Part of Batt'n moved from Barracks to Dug outs in Ramparts - 3 officers visited Nue 60 Sector. Heavy shelling by Germans of Shrapnel Corner & batteries near that point.	C.S.Y

WAR DIARY
INTELLIGENCE SUMMARY. 12th Durham L.I.

Army Form C. 2118.

(Erase heading not required.)

Place	Date	Hour	Summary of Events and Information	Remarks and references to Appendices
Ypres	27/4/17		Fine day. Slight shelling of Ypres also Shrapnel Corner & Lille Gate. 5 officers visited the Right + Centre Batt'n trenches in Hill 60 sector. We relieved 13th D.L.I. in Zillebeke Sector. Relief completed by 11 p.m. We took over more ground on our left viz the Warrington Ave + Lovers Lane up to Gap A. The companies were disposed as follows. "A" Coy on Right: Vancouver St. Front line from St. Peter's St. to Cross St. Supports in Gas Crawl + Winnipeg St. from St. Peter's St. to Crab Crawl. 3 platoons in all. "B" Coy. 1 Platoon in Winnipeg St - 1 in Hill St + 1 in Fort St - 3 platoons in all. "C" Coy. 1 Platoon .. Hill 60th St. 1 in Crew Trench + 1 in Support in Winnipeg St. 3 Plats. "D" Coy. 1 .. .. Lovers Walk + 2 in Warrington Ave: All Coys had one platoon on detached duties with Tunnelling Coys.	CEC
Zillebeke	28/4/17		Slight shelling of Winnipeg St + Vigo St. The HQrs of B Coy in Vigo street were shelled with 8 hy tomps in the morning. Casualties 3 Men wounded. Considerable aeroplane activity over German lines our planes being shelled. Zillebeke Village shelled with about 20 - 5.9's no damage to HQrs.	CEC

Army Form C. 2118.

WAR DIARY
or
INTELLIGENCE SUMMARY.
(Erase heading not required.)

12th Durham L.I.

Instructions regarding War Diaries and Intelligence Summaries are contained in F. S. Regs., Part II. and the Staff Manual respectively. Title pages will be prepared in manuscript.

Place	Date	Hour	Summary of Events and Information	Remarks and references to Appendices
Zillebeke Trenches	29/4/17		Very fine day. Party of Officers & NCOs from 9th Cheshires came to look over line, they relieve the Battⁿ on the 30th inst. Considerable activity in the air, one of our planes came down behind Lone Trench Observer & Pilot both wounded from. The machine was heavily shelled by Germans & both pictures, but both stretcher bearers Pte Olsen were brought in. The pilot had his leg broken but our stretcher bearers Pte Olsen & Pte Woodward of D Coy with Serg Gee & Proctor Capt Scott R.A.M.C. got him in. 1 O.R. killed & 1 O.R. wounded under a heavy considerable fire from snipers & guns.	O.C.
"	30/4/17		Very fine – Battⁿ after Vince St & Zillebeke St. Communication trenches shelled well between 9.30 am & also during day and shelling by T.M's of Winnipeg St. Battⁿ after relief moves to Steenvoorde area. Battⁿ relieved by 9th Cheshires. Billeting party went to Steenvoorde by motor.	C.E.C.
Steenvoorde 1/5/17 Area			Battⁿ relief completed at 1.30 am Battⁿ entrained Ypres sidings for Godeswaersvelde arriving 5 am where billeting party met Battⁿ. Companies moved to billets. Very scattered billets but comfortable.	

C.E. Cummins
Major
12th D.L.I.

WAR DIARY
or
INTELLIGENCE SUMMARY.
(Erase heading not required.)

Army Form C. 2118.

WD 2 O / '2' Durham L.I.

Place	Date	Hour	Summary of Events and Information	Remarks and references to Appendices
ZILLEBEKE Trenches.	1/5/17		Battalion was relieved by the 9th Cheshire Regt. Relief complete 1-30 AM. The Battalion entrained at YPRES siding at 3.35 am. & detrained at Godewaersvelde at 5 AM — marched to billets town about STEENVOORDE. Battalion rested all day.	M
STEENVOORDE AREA	2/5/17		Cleaning & refitting of equipment in view of GOC 23rd Div inspection. The Battalion was inspected by the Divisional Commander in field P.S. 0.02 at 4.30 p.m.	M
"	3/5/17	7 am 7.30 am 9.30 10.30	Physical drill — Company Commanders parade. Platoon Drill. Lewis Gunners under L.G. Officer. Signallers under Sig. Officer. The Battalion bathed at Steenvoorde in the afternoon & evening.	M
"	4/5/17	7 am 7.30 am 9 am 1 pm	Physical drill etc under Coy Comdr. Platoons practised in the attack of small localities or strong points, small schemes were set which Platoon Comdrs had to work out with Tactical Exer. action & inspections criticised	C.S.C.

Army Form C. 2118.

WAR DIARY
or
INTELLIGENCE SUMMARY.
(Erase heading not required.)

12th Dunham L.J.

Instructions regarding War Diaries and Intelligence Summaries are contained in F. S. Regs., Part II. and the Staff Manual respectively. Title pages will be prepared in manuscript.

Place	Date	Hour	Summary of Events and Information	Remarks and references to Appendices
Skindwoorde Area	5/5/17		Early. Usual work in morning from 9am-1pm. Coy's carried out similar work that of platoons yesterday. Conference of Officers after the works had been done.	CC
"	6/5/17		Church Parade in morning. M.O. inspected Batt⁵ in afternoon.	C.S.C.
"	7/5/17		Batt⁵ did Coy drill by Coy's during morning. A divisional Contact Aeroplane Scheme carried out on Training Area between Skindwoorde & Abeele. 8 Officers & all signallers Runners attended for instruction	C.S.C.
"	8/5/17		Batt⁵ carried out an attack over "A" Training Area near Skindwoorde In Conjunction with 1 section of 66th M.G.C. & 68th T.M.B. Batt⁵ ret'd to billets by 2pm. Orders rec'd to move tomorrow.	
Skindwoorde & Montreal Camp	9/5/17		Batt⁵ moved by road with Transport at 9.30 am to Montreal Camp near Ypres. Very hot & trying march for men arrived Camp 2.45 pm. Orders rec'd for Batt⁵ to take over from 8th Gloucester Reg⁵ the Hill 60 Centre Sub-Sector 5 Officers & 5 N.C.O.'s went forward to take over & they remain there until Batt⁵ arrives in Heavy bombardment on the Right Sector of Hill 60 line by the Germans.	C.S.C.

WAR DIARY
or
INTELLIGENCE SUMMARY.
(Erase heading not required.)

Army Form C. 2118.

12th Durham L.I.

Place	Date	Hour	Summary of Events and Information	Remarks and references to Appendices
Montreal Camp Hill 60 Entr	10/5/17		Very hot. Batt" preparing for trenches. 5 Officers & 4 N.C.O's per Coy went forward to reconnoitre & later in day 2 Lewis Guns & their teams with 28 men to take over advance post went forward under 2nd Lieut Niez. Packs were left behind at Transport. Batt" parade 9-15 p.m & marched to Vlamertinghe - the train being 1 hour late the Batt" did not entrain until 11 p.m & arrived at Ypres 11-20. Guides met Batt" at Lille Gate & Batt" moved to the line.	
Hill 60 Sub Sector	11/5/17		Relief Complete at 3.30 am. The line is held as follows:— D. Coy from Railway Cutting to I.29.C.6.2½ to Allan Post at I.29.C.9.5. The line consists of 3 advance post viz Marshall Post, Supt Post & Allan post & is in a very damaged condition, as this line was recently shelly before & had sapper received an intense bombardment. The remainder of D Coy are in Deep Support Trench to Allen St which runs in rear of the posts. The Left Coy "B" Coy from Allan Post I.29.C.9.5 to I.29.B.4.8 This sector is also held by Posts 3 in number viz No 13 Fosse Way Post, No Allen Crater Post I.29.D.1.6, Barry Post I.29.D.2½.9½, Glasgow Post	

WAR DIARY or INTELLIGENCE SUMMARY

Army Form C. 2118.

Place	Date	Hour	Summary of Events and Information	Remarks and references to Appendices
Hill 60 Sub Sector	11/5/17		Continued Glasgow Post. I.29-B-7.2. This portion of the line is in a similar condition to that on the right. A Coy are in close support but provide at night garrisons for 3 Posts viz. Lone Tree Post I.29.B.4.3. Fosse Wood Post I.29.B.2.4. & Fosse Way Post I.29.B.4.6 with Coy H.Qrs remainder of Coy in Dug outs at Battersea Farm in Fosse Way Trench. The Reserve Coy "C" are in the Dug outs at Larch Wood I-29-C-2-7 where Batt. H.Qrs & M.O. are accommodated. The M.A. Post is also in this Dug out system. Very fine day — On the whole very quiet. "MARSHALL WALK" dug MARSHALL Post, Dug Support, Battersea Farm shelters. All orders to supply as many men as possible to any assembly trenches — therefore work on improvement of own trenches & wire ceases.	C.E.C.
"	12/5/17			
	13/5/17		Enemy Artillery rather active in the morning — Cavalry Barracks, MARSHALL WALK & MARSHALL Post receives usual attention by Enemy. Strip Bange V	VB
			although a quiet afternoon.	

Army Form C. 2118.

WAR DIARY
or
INTELLIGENCE SUMMARY. /2st Durham L.I.
(Erase heading not required.)

Instructions regarding War Diaries and Intelligence Summaries are contained in F. S. Regs., Part II. and the Staff Manual respectively. Title pages will be prepared in manuscript.

Place	Date	Hour	Summary of Events and Information	Remarks and references to Appendices
Hill 60 Ante Sebastos	13/5/17	(cont)	A few minnies fell in the vicinity of COMPANY Trenches. Our Artillery carried on with the usual trench bombardment. The cutting of the enemy's wire was continued.	
			The day was quiet on the whole – Enemy were shelling on track area. Drawing received about	
do	14/5	4.0 pm	that an air photo discloses a new enemy trench – connecting the OLD CAIRO opposite MARSHALL POST & SWIFT POST, Higher Authority thought that this area & an assembly trench from which the enemy intended to raid us. Mr. Arthur our advanced posts & our Heavy Artillery bombarded it for 1½ hours. As soon as it was dark 3 Patrols were sent out from three different parts of the line. The patrols crossed ½ officer & 2 OR each. The patrols proceeded returned (see sketch map attached). There was absolutely no signs of any new trench.	

A6945 Wt. W11422/M1160 350,000 12/16 D. D. & L. Forms/C./2118/14.

WAR DIARY
or
INTELLIGENCE SUMMARY. /2 Durham L.I
(Erase heading not required.)

Army Form C. 2118.

Place	Date	Hour	Summary of Events and Information	Remarks and references to Appendices
Hill 60 entire sector	15/5/17		Our Artillery continued to cut wire cooperating with our medium. Enemy shelled deep support, MARSHALL WALK. Casualties 2 killed 8 wounded.	
"	16/5/17		Gas and Oil Shelling on both right & left Battalion Front Line. Received orders that the 11th N.F. were making a surprise raid on the Enemy trench. This operation was to form a balloon in relation to our	Ap.
"	17/5/17		Enemy shelled LARCHWOOD + CUTTING in retaliation to our heavy Trench Mortar firing on Enemy line. At 10.0 pm we had informed that he was going to blow a new mine near Hill 60 at 7.0 pm. before a Special party was relieved from B.Co. under 2/Lt Duffy to occupy the Crater if formed. At firing of the mine hun postpone until 10.0 pm. At 9.15 pm the enemy opens a heavy bombardment on our front supported line - especially concentrating on machine wall recently S.O.S. Signals were sent by someone in the right Battalion & as SOS signal were repeated from this Battalion HQs. as our guns	Ap.

WAR DIARY or INTELLIGENCE SUMMARY

Army Form C. 2118.

B. Dunham

Place	Date	Hour	Summary of Events and Information	Remarks and references to Appendices
Hill 60	17/5/17	(cont)	Were "standing to" for the explosion of our mine in the evening, brought one blow on the Enemy's line ahead immediately as will the own line – the enemy evidently intended to send us. The mine exploded at 10.10 pm & Sects 2 & 8 with Bombers advanced to establish a post in the Crater (of mine). There were no craters formed consequently the patrols & a no. to bombing the German Craters which were hurled by enemy to stop our firing & moving up to the German Craters & being mainly retired to our front trench. Bombers on patrol & being followed by the Germans. 2nd Lt Duff advanced to organize his platoon & was struck in his limb. Everything has quiet at midnight. Our casualties during the mine operation were 2 Killed 3 wounded and 1 man wounded & missing.	
	18/5/17		Early morning was exceptionally quiet – in the afternoon enemy shell MARSHALL WALK LATCHWOOD & the cutting – then the	

MARSHALL WALK LATCHWOOD

WAR DIARY
or
INTELLIGENCE SUMMARY.
(Erase heading not required.)

Army Form C. 2118.

12 Durham 1

Place	Date	Hour	Summary of Events and Information	Remarks and references to Appendices
Hill 60 and surrounds		(Cont'd) 16/5/17	fire being intense at times - especially front to the right of the railway in S.P.9. Our 18 pdr & medium Trench Mortars continued to cut enemy wire opposite the "Snout" & Manstead Post. At night our Machine Guns continued on Gaps in Enemy wire - at times our M.G's were firing about erratically 1 Sect who was about to go to fire patrol were killed on our own fire step. An officer & patrol went out from Snipers Post to endeavour to find the missing men of the previous evenings operations. The Battalion was relieved by 8th YORKSHIRE REGT. relief complete at 1-30 A.M. The Battalion marched back to MONTREAL CAMP & arriving there about 4.0 A.M. (19th)	AG —
MONTREAL CAMP	19/5/17		Our total casualties during the tour was 10 Killed & 32 wounded) Battalion rested all day in MONTREAL CAMP. About 9am an A.A. Shell fell through the roof of one hut & wounded two men.	D

WAR DIARY
or
INTELLIGENCE SUMMARY.

(Erase heading not required.)

Army Form C. 2118.

Place	Date	Hour	Summary of Events and Information	Remarks and references to Appendices
MONTREAL CAMP	20/5/17		Battalion in MONTREAL Camp. Supplying Working parties to R.E. daily. About 200 men present daily.	
	26/5/17		Left MONTREAL CAMP 3 a.m. marched to EECKE in	
EECKE	27/5/17		Billets arriving about 8.30 a.m. the Battalion being attached to 69th Brigade for training and practice grounds. Battalion were at rest all day.	
"	28/5/17		C.O. Coy Commdrs & Signallers went to Steenvoorde then Sect 27. 15.22.c to look on & observe practice trenches. Remainder of Battalion did Gas Helmet drill.	
	29/5/17		Battalion paraded at 7 a.m. marched to Steenvoorde & saw practice attack and Battalion into the whole 69th Bde did practice advance. Returned to billets about 4.0 p.m.	
	30/5/17		Brigade training on STEENVOORDE Trng area. Battalion returned to Billets about 2.30 p.m.	

WAR DIARY
or
INTELLIGENCE SUMMARY.
(Erase heading not required.)

Army Form C. 2118.

Place	Date	Hour	Summary of Events and Information	Remarks and references to Appendices
ECKE & RAILWAY DUGOUTS.	31/5		Receive orders to proceed to the line with 68 Inf. Bde. Rests on way - passed at 8 pm through to GODEWAERSVELDE Station. Entrained for Ypres at 9-30 p.m. Battalion detrained at Ypres Siding at 11-30 p.m. - good deal of shelling going on or Relieved "G" Yorks stance in RAILWAY DUGOUTS & BUND. dug complete at 12 1-0 A.M. 1/6/17.	M.

Bott
Capt rank of OC
12 Durham. LI

WAR DIARY
or
INTELLIGENCE SUMMARY.
(Erase heading not required.)

Army Form C. 2118.

68 Vol 21
/23 Durham Light Infantry

Place	Date	Hour	Summary of Events and Information	Remarks and references to Appendices
RAILWAY DUGOUTS near YPRES	1/6/17		Battalion established in this position. The Railway Dugouts were heavily shelled all day - about 20 casualties resulting. 400 men furnished for working parties under R.E.	
	2/6		Usual steady making parties provided	A
	3/6		Not very much work on the whole. The enemy fires a slight number of gas shells which caused some annoyance	A
	4/6		Very warm day. About 5 pm we were informed the 15th "W" day 10 June day before zero hour to be Second Army 6 Memoir. The Battalion was relieved by the 10 West Riding Regt - on completion of relief the Battalion moved to the Ramparts Bryant YPRES	A
	5/6/17		Made all preparation for the attack - the whole operation being carefully explained to the men. Conference of officers in the afternoon.	A

WAR DIARY or INTELLIGENCE SUMMARY

Army Form C. 2118.

1/2 D Durham L.I

Place	Date	Hour	Summary of Events and Information	Remarks and references to Appendices
RAMPARTS YPRES	6/17		During the day men were as quiet as possible. At 10 p.m. the Battalion moved off to take up any position ready for the attack. Attacked as per Opns. Order in position at 12-30 AM. (7th)	
ZILLEBEKE SWITCH	7/17		At 1 AM informed that Zero hour would be 3-10 a.m. At 3 AM all was peaceful - everyone lay out in the open waiting for the men to appear. Promptly at 3-10 AM 'Up' went the mine - when the most intense Bombardment the enemy line commenced - the enemy barrage also opening out immediately. The Battalion lay out in the open until 4-30 when we moved up to our second position. Our Objectives was gained by 7-30 AM with only 15 Casualties. The Cavalries on position taken 12 noon the enemy aeroplanes 'spotted' our new	

WAR DIARY
or
INTELLIGENCE SUMMARY.
(Erase heading not required.)

Army Form C. 2118.

12 Durham L.I.

Place	Date	Hour	Summary of Events and Information	Remarks and references to Appendices
T.36.b.1.3. to 6	7/7	(cont.)	patrols. Consequently shells of all calibre fell in our	
T.36.c.2.5. (sheet 28)			own trench. Our casualties are totalling up very rapidly. By 6.0 p.m. our casualties had amounted to over 200 not including about 50 men missing. The guns which were enfilading our Crawnelles came from our left front – in front of the VIII Corps, when our reports to the 69 Brigade but the enemy shelling never ceased. The line we held was from T.36.B.1.3 to T.36.c.2.5.	DD
do	8/7		2d Battalion was relieved by 13 Durham L.I. at 1 am – moving to BATTERSEA FARM & neighbouring trenches with the exception of "D" intermille shelling here – the men had a rest.	DD
Authuille farm	9/7		12 Battalion moved to MONTROSE Camp H.19. (sheet 20) new billets – finished all day. He were informed by Gen Babington that we were go back to the line on the night of the 10th / 11th	DD
do	10/7		rest all day – at night relieved the 10 West Riding at Battle	

WAR DIARY
or
INTELLIGENCE SUMMARY.
(Erase heading not required.)

Army Form C. 2118.

12 Durham L.I.

Place	Date	Hour	Summary of Events and Information	Remarks and references to Appendices
Battle Wood	10/6/17		Wood. Their final Objective has not been gained before the Baln.	
"	11/6/17		Rifle fire was not very close. But the whole of the day was very quiet, about it an Enemy aeroplane flew very low over our line firing into our trenches with M.Gs. At night the enemy kept up a barrage on our lines & expended between our New & our front line.	MD
	12/6/17		Supper line. Much quiet — nothing of importance occurred	MD
	13/6/17		In the afternoon enemy shelled our forward positions heavily. N.C.V. Three wounded from other Officers Losses. At night we were relieved by the 3 R.B. — but before doing so we gained the "Black" Objective without any Artillery preparation. This we handed over to the 3rd R.B. — but they refused to take	MS
	14/6/17		has it. Relief was not complete until following morning. Relief complete at 4-30 am Battalion marched over this railway to Kanacafe where in entrained. Enemy hurt up	MD

WAR DIARY
or
INTELLIGENCE SUMMARY.
(Erase heading not required.)

Army Form C. 2118.

12 "Durham L.I."

Place	Date	Hour	Summary of Events and Information	Remarks and references to Appendices
	14/6/17	(Cont.)	a Gas Barrage between YPRES & our Sec Front Line — Battalion worked thro' it without casualties. Entrained at Godwaersvelde & marched to the BERTHEN Area	AB
BERTHEN AREA	15/17/6		Arriving in Camp at 8 am	
	20/17		Battalion in BERTHEN Area — Bns for Coys training daily viz — Musketry — Lewis Gun — Bombing — Bayonet — Battalion. Lieut. C.S. Cunningham 2/5th proceeded to take Command of 11" Royal Sussex Regt. — Lt. Col. Lynam was on leave to England	AB
	21/17		Battalion proceeded by Motor lorry to DICKEBUSCH area & took up K X Corps Supplies. 350 men daily for work near Hill 60 for X Corps Supplies.	AB
	22/6 to 25/6		Supplying work parties for X Corps Signals. The enemy shelled our Camp every night. One horse was killed by an AA shell.	AB
	26/6		Battalion proceeded to FLETRE (Shed 27) by Motor lorry arriving in Camp about 1.0 PM. Men rested all day	AB

WAR DIARY
or
INTELLIGENCE SUMMARY. 12 Durham L.I.

Army Form C. 2118.

Place	Date	Hour	Summary of Events and Information	Remarks and references to Appendices
METRE (Sheet 27)	27/17		The Divisional Commander presents Ribbons to the men	
			Officers trained with	
			Operations in 2nd Army Offensive then also Bathes	AB
	28th		Battalion route marches about 9 miles. Players cricket match	AB
			In the Evening	
	29/17		Musketry & handling of arms through inspection of	AB
			Small Kit	
	30/17		The whole Brigade marches to MIC MAC CAMP nr DICKEBUSCH	AB
			relieving the 2nd Division. Rained very hard all day.	

D. Scott
Capt Acting
12 DLI

5. DISPOSITIONS Before and during Z day

'W' day.   In the line.
W/X. night.   YPRES.
X/Y night.   YPRES.
Y/Z. night.   To left support i.e. "C" & "D" coys in LARCH WOOD Subway, & "A" & "B" coys in fields at I.22.d., north of FOSSE WAY Battⁿ H. Qrs. ZILLEBEKE SWITCH.

6. FORMATIONS IN ATTACK ETC.

The assault up to the BLUE LINE will be made (on the front allotted to the Battⁿ) by the 11th West Yorks Regt. on the left & part of the 8th Yorks Regt. on the Right.

The 12th D.L.I. will pass through these Battⁿˢ at the BLUE LINE and continue the assault up to the BLACK LINE. It will pass the BLUE LINE at ZERO + 3 hours 40 minutes.

Coys. will leave their support positions (as detailed in PARA.5) in time to occupy the following positions at ZERO + 1 hour and 50 minutes.

"A" coy. in WANGARATA TRENCH & COMPANY TRENCH.
"C" coy. in DEEP SUPPORT & COMPANY TRENCH, point of Junction about I.29.c.9.7.
"B" coy. in X TRENCH & METROPOLITAN LEFT with its Right at ZILLEBEKE SWITCH
"D" coy. in METROPOLITAN LEFT with its Left at ZILLEBEKE SWITCH and its right in METROPOLITAN RIGHT.

The advance from these positions will commence at ZERO + 2 hours and 20 minutes. These positions will be taken up and the advance commenced without any further orders from O.C. Battⁿ.

The formations adopted for the advance must depend on circumstances, but from the start to the German 1st Line trenches the diamond formation will probably be found most suitable. From here onwards the normal formation of 4 waves will probably be the best.

Distances between Lines 20 yards, between Waves 50 yards and between Companies 100 yards.

It may, however, be found advisable to work up the German Communication trenches.

The 9th Yorks Regt. will assault the BLACK LINE south of the Railway at the same time as the 12th D.L.I. assault the BLACK LINE north of the Railway.

1 coy. of the 8th Yorks Regt. will co-operate at the same time to keep touch between the above 2 battⁿˢ

6. cont'd. this Company will move down the Railway and in particular clear and consolidate the dug outs in RAILWAY CUTTING.

If an attack is held up at any point which is not likely to cause more than a temporary obstruction, information is to be at once sent to Batt'n H.Qrs. giving careful information as to the point or points on the enemy's front which is causing the obstruction, a special 45 minutes bombardment will be arranged for, the last 5 minutes of which will be intense.

7. CONSOLIDATION. The BLACK LINE is to be consolidated at once and strongly held, posts being pushed forward to cover the work of consolidation and strong patrols pushed forward to IMPERFECT TRENCH to ascertain if it is held, every platoon, every section and as far as possible everyman must be given a definite point to reach & work to do in each objective to be attacked. Moppers up at the rate of 6 per platoon will be allotted exact areas to clear and must be given definite routes. Lewis Gun Sections and Bomb Sections must also be given definite objects to reach and convert into strong points as quickly as possible, the determination to reach his personal objective and to consolidate it at all costs must be impressed on every man.

8. DRESS & EQUIPMENT In accordance with S.S. 135 Section 31. & as already communicated verbally.

9. Numbers to go into ACTION. In accordance with S.S. 135 Section 30. Officers and other ranks left behind will proceed to the Brigade re-inforcement camp (which is at the old Transport Lines) at a time to be specified later.

10. RATIONS & WATER
W. day. Normal.
X. day Normal.
Y/Z night. To be drawn from dump at YPRES for consumption on Z day.
Z/A night. To be drawn from dump at LARCH WOOD for consumption on "A" day.
Rations for Z day will be issued to the men before the assault commences.

10. contd.

Water can be obtained at STREAM CORNER & at a point on the VERBRANDEN ROAD, I.21.D.9.0. & in addition to these supplies 100 full petrol tins will be kept at LARCH WOOD for the Battⁿ but this reserve is not to be touched except by order of O/C. Battⁿ.

The urgency for saving Water tins and returning them to the nearest water point to be refilled must be impressed on all ranks, the greatest care is to be taken in filling the Water bottles and to this end funnels will be issued later.

The urgency of conserving the water must also be strongly impressed on all ranks.

Every man going to the objective from the rear must start with a full water bottle.

11. FORWARD COMMAND POST.

At I.29.d.60.05. This will be established by the Battⁿ Sig. Officer who with his men will leave Battⁿ. H.Qrs 1 hour after the capture of the RED OBJECTIVE. He will report direct to the Brigade directly the post is established and will send a runner back to Battⁿ. H.Qrs. to act as guide for the C.O.

Waiting Stokes Gunners & Machine Gunners will assist in making this post until called on for their own work.

12. STOKES MORTARS.

Two Stokes Mortars under an Officer will be attached to the Battⁿ. These two Mortars will remain at the FORWARD COMMAND POST till wanted. 1 Stokes Gunner will be attached to each of the leading Coys. & will be used as a runner to bring up the guns when wanted. Officers Commdg. the advance Coys. will send back one of their men with the Stokes Mortar runner when the guns are called for, to assist in directing the guns to the required positions. Officers Commdg. the leading Coys. will send to the FORWARD COMMAND POST on their own initiative.

The Stokes Mortar Amm. Dump is at LARCH WOOD.

13. MACHINE GUNS & STRONG POINTS

By Corps orders a Strong Point will be made at E.35.B.9.2. in addition to any others that may be required. O/C "C" Coy will detail 1 Platoon to construct and hold this strong point and will make arrangements for carrying up his own material to be drawn from LARCH WOOD DUMP.

2 Machine Guns are detailed to assist in holding this point, these will remain at the FORWARD COMMAND POST until wanted, arrangements similar to that of the Stokes Mortars (see Para 12) are to be made for the sending for these guns.

The O/C. M.G. Section will detail such of his men as can be spared to assist in preparing positions for these Guns.

14. STRAGGLERS POSTS

Stragglers posts will be established as follows.
No 1. Post at I.13.c.25.85. Middle of KRUISSTRAAT.
" 2 Post at H.18.D.0.0. near BELGIAN CHATEAU

O/C Coys will insure that all men leaving the Battle field for any reason including lightly wounded will take back with them their rifle & equipment.

15. CONTACT AEROPLANE.

1. Contact Aeroplanes will be up from ZERO if light enough till ZERO + 6 hours, it will be distinguished by 3 broad white bands on the body & by the attachment of a black board on the lower left plane.

This aeroplane will call for flares by firing a White Very Light and sounding the Klaxon Horn, the leading infantry will light flares approximately at the following times

ZERO + 30 minutes
ZERO. + 1 hour.
ZERO. + 4 hours- 30 mins
ZERO + 6 hours

These flares will be lighted in sets of 3 and tied together if possible. Infantry must however insure that the plane is calling for flares before lighting up.

Isolated bodies of troops out of touch on the flanks should light flares when called upon to do so.

15 contd.   A Wireless Aeroplane will be up during the day to look for counter attacks, and will warn the infantry of such attacks by means of a Red Flare, this machine will also transmit infantry messages calling for Barrage.

16.
R.E. DUMPS

Material for consolidation at
GRAND FLEET STREET - I.34.B.4.9.
LARCH WOOD.   I.29.C.3.8.
VERRETT RIDE.   I.29.A.8.2.
ALLEN CRATER.

S.AA.
GRENADES
BOMBS
ETC.

S.AA. Grenades, BOMBS, VERY LIGHTS etc.
LARCH WOOD.
GRAND FLEET STREET. - I.34.B.5.8.
BENSHAM ROAD.
VERRETT RIDE.   I.29.A.9.0.
ALLEN STREET.
METROPOLITAN LEFT.
SUNKEN ROAD.

17.
MAPS &
DOCUMENTS

No Maps, plans, diaries, private letters, documents or papers of any description which might afford information to the enemy are to be taken into action by any one, with the exception of the Message Map 14. scale 10,000 and the Trench Map Hill 60. Scale 5,000.

18.
MEDICAL
ARRANGEMENTS

Regt. Aid Post in LARCH WOOD.
There will be 8 Stretcher Bearers per Coy. who will go forward with their Coys. If Coys. cannot find 8 trained men they must make up the number with untrained men.
The Auxiliary Stretcher bearers must be unarmed and wear the armlets.

R.V. Tyndall
Lieut. Colonel,
Commanding 12th Battalion The
Durham Light Infantry

MAP 14

Scale 1:10,000.

M A P V I.

To 23rd Division.   No. ....
                                (Note:- Either give Map Reference)
                                (or mark your position by a "X"on)
1. I am at .... (the Map on Back.)

2. I have reached First(Red)
             Second(Blue) Objective.
             Third(Black)

3. I am at .... and am consolidating

4. I am at .... and have consolidated.

5. Am held up by (a) M.G.
                 (b) Wire. at ....(Place where you are)

6. Enemy holding strong point ....

7. I am in touch with .... on Right at ....
                                            Left.

8. I am not in touch with .... on Right
                                          Left.

9. Am shelled from ....

10. I need:- (a) S.A. Ammunition.
             (b) Bombs.
             (c) Rifle Grenades.
             (d) Water.
             (e) Very Lights.
             (f) Stokes Shells.

11. Counter Attack forming at ....

12. Hostile (a) Battery   )
            (b) Machine Gun   ) active at ....
            (c) Trench Mortar)

13. Reinforcements wanted at ....

14. I estimate my present strength at .... rifles.

                        Name ....
Time .... m   Platoon ....
Date ....1917.   Company ....
                        Battalion ....

68/23

Vol 2 Army Form C. 2118.
1/2 Durham L.I.

WAR DIARY
or
INTELLIGENCE SUMMARY.
(Erase heading not required.)

Place	Date	Hour	Summary of Events and Information	Remarks and references to Appendices
McMAC CAMP	1/7/17		Battalion in MICMAC CAMP. Thorough inspection of Steel Helmets, Gas Masks, Zillo Bivouac Sh. Etc. Clean Camp. Enemy Shells never about the Camp - one Shell dropping near to transport lines.	
McKIBRUCK	2/7/17	1-30 pm	Camp terribly Shelled for an hour - two casualties.	
			Staff of No O.R. arrives. Very good except.	
	3/7/17		A few shells over Bde Headquarters in morning.	
	4/7/17		Bon paraded to see H.R.H. King George along the — at 9.15 am. The King — Prince of Wales drove along slowly in two cars.	
	5/7/17		To day the division (23rd) was transferred to II Second Corps 5th Army and the 69th Bde went into the line from KLEIN ZILLEBEKE to CRAB CRAWL	
	6/7/17		In MICMAC CAMP, a working party, and only a few shells near Bde Headquarters,	
	7/7/17			
16	8/7/17		Relieved 13th DLI in trenches from Klein Zillebeke	

WAR DIARY
or
INTELLIGENCE SUMMARY

(Erase heading not required.)

Army Form C. 2118.

Place	Date	Hour	Summary of Events and Information	Remarks and references to Appendices
KLEIN ZILLEBEKE			15 DAVIDSON STREET. Fairly quiet night. Front line shelled lightly in morning. No casualties; men fairly secure in concrete Boche Dugouts.	
	11.7.17			
	12.7.17		Raid by 10 men of B Coy and covering flank parties consisting of Lieut. Weishman & 20 Freemen. Fairly under charge of Lieut. Sterling point at T.36. 6 & 4. with completed successes. 5 prisoners taken, dead & eight men and 6 men were wounded. Three men reported missing.	
	13.7.17		Relieved by 9th Bn. Rif. Brigade. Bn. marched back to MICMAC CAMP SOUTH.	
	14.7.17		Bn. at rest in hut MICMAC CAMP. Only one working party.	
	16.7.17		Companies on musketry, gas drill and P.T. &B.F. all morning. Baths in afternoon.	
	20.7.17		Bn. marched via Berthen to camp between FLETRE and METEREN.	

WAR DIARY
or
INTELLIGENCE SUMMARY.
(Erase heading not required.)

Army Form C. 2118.

Place	Date	Hour	Summary of Events and Information	Remarks and references to Appendices
	28/7/17	about 3 p.m.	Inspection by General Babington - G.O.C. Division in morning. From his date 6th to 28th the Battalion remained at rest within camp. Parades consisted chiefly of musketeering, gas drill and company and platoon pack work. Every man within Battalion fired 20 rounds at 15 yd range. On the afternoon of the 28th Brigade sports were held, which includes horse jumping, lecture, cross ties etc.	
	29/7/17		Bn. marched Bn. at 11.45 am to CAESTRE entraining at 3 p.m. for St Omer. Arrived St Omer at about 8 p.m. and marched to billets at ESQUERDES arriving at 11.30 p.m., very comfortable billets for the whole Battalion.	
	30/7/17		Owing to rain there were no parades this day.	

WAR DIARY
INTELLIGENCE SUMMARY. 1/2 Durham L.I.

Vol 23

Army Form C. 2118.

Place	Date	Hour	Summary of Events and Information	Remarks and references to Appendices
ESQUERDES	1.8.17		In Billets at ESQUERDES. The Battalion was out every day on the training ground near SETQUES where there were plenty of short rifle range & ground for training, training rifle grenades.	
	6.8.17			WRH
	7.8.17		The Battalion marched to Billets at SERQUES & came under the Commans of G.O.C. XVIII Corps for training. Practising for the attack was carried on much in the same way as at ESQUERDES, but there were not the same facilities for training	WRH
	9.8.17			
	10.8.17		Battalion Bathes at ST OMER but arranges from Billets to Lumien.	WRH
	11.8.17		Battalion on training area all day. All Infantry Officers proceed under the CO for childrens practices.	WRH
	12.8.17		Church parades at 1pm the Battalion march to the Rifle range at the training area.	WR2
	13.8.17		One Platoon from C Coy proceeds on a Musketry course at	

Army Form C. 2118.

WAR DIARY
or
INTELLIGENCE SUMMARY.
(Erase heading not required.)

12 Durham Light Infy

Place	Date	Hour	Summary of Events and Information	Remarks and references to Appendices
NORTHCOURT	13.6.17		71467 Manus & No 53529 Cpl Stokey Ist Reserves accompanied the party no instruction Ranks of course	
			be various - 300 159 Cpl Rippon M. - It 1st Class Shots - 13	
			2nd Class Shots 7. 3rd class shots	M.
ST. OVES	14.6.17		Gas demonstration at EPERLEQUES. 2 OR per Coy attended.	M.
	15.6.17		Battalion in training area. A bonus for Officer commenced at VOLKERINGHOVE - prior to camp. Eight Officers attended.	
			N° 15344 Pte P. Smith was tried by F.G.C.M. 9 am R.S. Company	
			Church parade in Church at EPERQUES.	M.
	16.6.17		Route march - cookers accompanied Coys. Practise Scheme by Battalion in training area. Copy of Scheme attached.	M.
			A Scabies Inspection was held by M.O. in the evening.	M.
	17.6.17		Officer & N.C.O. proceeded to view Model trenches near BEAVEREN. Battalion marched to TRAMP Area - being relieved at same relieve arriving there via York Camp. Gas Lecture via Esquir began at 6 p.m	M.

WAR DIARY
or
INTELLIGENCE SUMMARY.
(Erase heading not required.)

Army Form C. 2118.

Place: 12 Durham Light Infantry

Date	Hour	Summary of Events and Information	Remarks and references to Appendices
16/8/17		Major A.B. Dick-Cleland, 2/Lt Freeman M.S. & 2/Lt Proctor proceeded to Eurainus Rienforcement Camp HOUTKERQUE and employed on staff.	
	6-15 a.m.	Gas alert. Battalion fired on "B" range near Kuning area.	No
		Church Parade; a conference of all officers was held on the School room SERQUES at 2.0 p.m.	No
19/8/17			No
20/8/17	6-30 A.M.	Bno Drill. Battalion took part in Brigade scheme on the training area. Capt N.C.A. Gau was provided where to enemy. Eight hon were motorcar carrier pigeons at Bre HQ	No
21/8/17	6-30 A.M.	Bno drill. The Bno meets were actually when to have entrenched street never attacks. Camp at the chappelle. 1 Company Commr. Maj Banks at Houtle.	No
22/8/17		An platoon from A Coy proceeded to hourketz came at NORTHECOURT. Battalion took part in Brigade Exercise on training area	No

WAR DIARY
or
INTELLIGENCE SUMMARY.
(Erase heading not required.)

Army Form C. 2118.

Instructions regarding War Diaries and Intelligence Summaries are contained in F. S. Regs., Part II. and the Staff Manual respectively. Title pages will be prepared in manuscript.

/2 Battalion

Place	Date	Hour	Summary of Events and Information	Remarks and references to Appendices
SERQUES	22/8/17	6-30 am	Bgde Gen drill Coy at the disposal of Coy Comdrs. At 8. Coy. proceeded to Rifle Range. Lewis Gunner taking their usual as TOURNEHEM. Lewis Gun teams had practice firing their Guns. The Transport moved off by route march to POPERINGHE AREA now to OUDERDOM (Rhens de Belgus) halts at NOORDPEENE for the night the following morning to Audenarm.	/As
	24/8/17		Gen parade Jan. Battalion left Billets at 6 p.m. marches to WATTEN Station but did not entrain until 1-30 am (25th)	/As
CORNWALL CAMP G-30 A.5.6	25/8/17		Battalion detrained at RENINGHELST at 7-30 am marches to CORNWALL CAMP near OUDERDOM arriving at 8-15 am. Battalion rested all day	/As
	26/8/17		Church parade. Conference of Officers in HQ Mess at 2.0 p.m.	/As
	27/8/17		Battalion in Camp - 6-30 am Gas drill - 9-10 Handling arms	/As

A6945 Wt. W11422/M1160 35,000 12/16 D. D. & L. Forms/C./2118/14.

WAR DIARY
or
INTELLIGENCE SUMMARY.

Army Form C. 2118.

12 Brigade L.I.

Place	Date	Hour	Summary of Events and Information	Remarks and references to Appendices
CORNWALL CAMP	5/7/17	Col.O.	11-12 noon Platoon drill — 2-3 Bayonet fighting gunners & Lagrethe under the new instructor.	Rts
"	6/7/17		Officer this platoon proceeds to EcerE YPRES to be attached to 23rd Divisional Bombing Offrs. 6-30 a.m Gas drill — 11-12 Musketry. Exercise changes fighting.	
			9-10 Platoon drill	Rts
			2-3 Lectures. 7-30 a.m R.E. Church parade	
	7/7/17		5 men attacked to DIS' Employed Coy for duty as TROUGH WARDENS. The following were received from Catrol T.J Bencher RAMC + private in Battalion order. "I wrote to bring to your attention the gallant conduct of N° ROII Pte. C. Wordsworth 'D' Coy in going across to a patient in the Hospital (3 Can CCS) on 12.7.17"	
			Routine. 9-10 Coy drill. 11-12 Bombing practise 2-3 Lectures. All Lewis gunners under Sergeant Lewis Gun Instructor	Rts
			6-pm the Battalion marches to huts	
H26.B.5.8			in DICKEBUSCH AREA — taking over camp at H.26.B.5.8	Rts
DICKEBUSCH AREA				

Army Form C. 2118.

WAR DIARY
or
INTELLIGENCE SUMMARY. 12 Anson L.I.
(Erase heading not required.)

Place	Date	Hour	Summary of Events and Information	Remarks and references to Appendices
H 26 B 5 8 DICKEBUSCH AREA	30/8		Camp thoroughly cleaned up. Gas parade 6-30 a.m. Remainder	
			of the day Company staff preparing for Coy Games 2 pm	
			Conference of Officers in HQ Mess	
			11-0 pm one shell fell in Camp killing one Horse.	M3
	31/8		100 Officer & Senior NCO's proceeded to reconnoitre positions in which	
			4 am Coy Offensive.	
			Gas Drill 6-30 am. Remainder of day Coys at the disposal	
			of Coy Comnd. Intensive musqy carried on. Rifle Inspection incl.	Ch
			2 Lt Nicholson	

W. Wyndowath Lt Colonel
Comdg 12" Anson L.I.

OPERATION ORDERS.

BY LIEUT-COLONEL R. TYNDALL.

FOR PRACTICE SCHEME TO BE CARRIED OUT ON TRAINING AREA. D. BY THE 12th. BATTALION THE DURHAM LIGHT INFANTRY.

Reference Map Sheet 27.a. S.E.

GENERAL IDEA.

The Germans are retiring in a South-Westerly direction, and on the evening of the 15th. August were known to be in position on the line INGLINGHAM - MORINGHAM.

SPECIAL IDEA.

The 12th. D. L. I. are to assault and consolidate that portion of the enemy' position between Q. 19. c. 4. 2. and Q. 19. c. 0. 8.

1. ZERO HOUR - 10.30 a.m.

2. Advance to be made from a starting point at least 1500 yards from the enemy's position.

3. Half the advance in diamond formation (by platoons) in three waves; one Company in the first wave, two in the second, and one in the third. (See Plan).

4. Second part of the advance in extended lines.

5. All available picks and shovels to be taken, and equally distributed among platoons, and Battalion Headquarters.

6. Intensive Digging for one hour to be done on enemy's position, Battalion Headquarters to dig in also.

7. Covering parties of small posts, i.e. a Lewis Gun and a few Riflemen to be pushed 200 yards beyond the line while it is being dug. These parties will dig in also.

D Drewery
a adj for.

Lieut-Colonel.
Commanding 12th. BATTALION THE DURHAM LIGHT INF.

August 15th. 1917.

Copy No., 1. - C.O.
2. - O.C. "A" Coy.
3. - O.C. "B" "
4. - O.C. "C" "
5. - O.C. "D" "
6. - File.

SECRET.   COPY NO.........

BRIGADE EXERCISE.
12th. BATTALION THE DURHAM LIGHT INFANTRY.

Ref., Map 27A., S.E. and   August 21st. 1917.
POELCAPPELLE, Sc. 1/10,000.

1.   Tomorrow, the 22nd., inst., the 68th. Infantry Brigade will
practice an attack over a piece of ground to represent an area
(Map POELCAPPELLE 1/10000) with the following boundaries. D.7.
Central to D.1.c.0.0. - Country Cross Roads - V.21.a.3.4. -
V.26.a.1.6. - WELLINGTON FARM (inclusive) - D.7. Central.

2.   The 11th. N.F. will attack the first objective (Blue Line).
       The 12th. D.L.I. will attack the second objective (Red Line)
with 3 Companies - one in reserve for carrying, viz. "A" Coy.
Right, "B" Coy. Centre, "D" Coy. Left - "C" Coy. Carrying.

       The 10th. N.F. and 13th. D.L.I. will attack the 3rd. or final
objective (Black Line) - the 10th. N.F. on the left and the 13th
D.L.I. on the Right.

3.   ZERO HOUR. - 9 a.m.

4.   OBJECTIVES.

       The first (or Blue Line), is the ground between Q.13.a.
Central and P.18.d.6.6. It represents a line on the POELCAPPELLE
map approx. from Wellington Farm to V. 26.c.0.0.
       The second, (or Red Line), is the road between P.13.c.2.7.
and P.12.d.3.2. It represents a line on the POELCAPPELLE map
approx. from WELLINGTON between D.3.a.1.6. and the country
cross-roads.
       The third (or black line) between P.16.b.7.9. and P.
11.b.1.7., which represents line between V.26.a.1.6. to
V.21.a.9.4.

       The 11th. N.F. will form up on a line Q.14.c.0.6. to
Q.20.a.0.3., ready to move to the attack at ZERO.

       The Barrage will lift at the rate of 100 yards in 5
minutes and will rest 200 yards beyond blue line for one hour.

       The Barrage will be denoted by flags, which will be
raised 100 yards every 5 minutes.

5.   The 12th. D.L.I. will be in position to move from the
blue line at ZERO Plus 2 Hours 5 minutes.
       The 13th. D.L.I. and 10th. N.F. will form up on the
Red Line, dividing line being the Cross Roads at P.18.a.8.6.
inclusive to the right Battalion.

       The Black Line will be divided at P.11.c.5.5.

       The Barrage will rest 200 yards beyond the Red Line
for one and a half hours.

6.   MACHINE GUNS.   Two Machine Guns from the M.G.Coy. will be under
the orders of O.C. 12th. D.L.I.
                Eight Machine Guns will be in Brigade Reserve at
Q.20.b.8.2.

7.   SIGNALLING. The Signalling Officer will make arrangements with
the Brigade Signalling Officer for Signal Communication between
Battalion and Brigade Headquarters.
       Brigade Headquarters will be at Q.20.d.5.1.

8.   AMMUNITION DUMP. Brigade Forward S.A.A. R.E. and Assistant Dumps
will be at Q.21.a. Central.

9. TOOLS. Will be carried as for Battalion Scheme yesterday, and will be issued by the Quartermaster this evening.

10. PACK ANIMALS. Will not go beyond Brigade Forward Dump.
The same arrangements will hold good for Transport as for the Scheme yesterday. Lewis Guns will be taken from the Wagons at the Rendezvous.

11. A new formation has been adopted for Platoons in the Attack. Copies of Instructions are being printed and will be issued later down to Platoon Commanders.

12. The Battalion will parade outside Battalion Headquarters, ready to march off at 8.45 a.m. DRESS. Same as for yesterday.

13. Digging will only take place in Stubble, and trenches dug will be filled in.

14. Watches will be synchronised at Battalion Headquarters at 9 p.m. to-night.

15. Without any further orders, the Battalion will be ready to move off from the starting point at ZERO plus 1 hr. 38 mins, crossing the blue line at ZERO plus 2 hours and 5 minutes.

(Signed). J. F. ROBB.

Capt. & Adjutant.
12th. Bn. THE DURHAM LIGHT INFANTRY.

Copy No., 1. Commanding Officer.
" " 2. O. C. "A" Coy.
" " 3. "   "B" "
" " 4. "   "C" "
" " 5. "   "D" "
" " 6. Transport Officer.
" " 7. Medical Officer.
" " 8. Signalling Officer.
" " 9. R. S. M.
" " 10. File.

CONFIDENTIAL.

WAR DIARY

of

12th(S) BATTALION, THE DURHAM LIGHT INFANTRY.

From. 1st Sept. 1917.

To. 30th Sept. 1917.

WAR DIARY
or
INTELLIGENCE SUMMARY.
(Erase heading not required.)

12th BN THE DURHAM LIGHT INFY.

Army Form C. 2118.

Place	Date	Hour	Summary of Events and Information	Remarks and references to Appendices
DICKEBUSCH AREA. CAMP AT H.24.b.5.8.	1/9/17		Battalion in camp in the DICKEBUSCH AREA. Coy at the disposal of C.R.E. Practice in extensive digging. Special exercise of rifle grenadiers; visit to model trenches in the afternoon by Platoon Commanders & NCO's.	
MICMAC CAMP A.21.b.5.5. about 2½ miles	2/9/17		Battalion moved by route march to MICMAC CAMP. Great enemy activity in the air after dark. Three bombs of heavy calibre were dropped in the vicinity of the camp, no damage was done. The Blenys were heavily engaged by our Anti Aircraft & aviators.	
"			Battalion in MICMAC CAMP. Companies at the disposal of C.R.E.	
STEENVOORDE AREA	3/9/17		Battalion moved by route march to STEENVOORDE AREA.	
"	4/9/17		Battalion in billets near STEENVOORDE. Companies at disposal of Company Commanders for inspectional etc.	
NOORDPEENE	5/9/17		Battalion moved by route march to billets at NOORDPEENE leaving about 4 a.m. & arriving about 12.30 a.m.	
"	6/9/17		Battalion in billets at NOORDPEENE. "A" "B" & "D" Companies section & platoon drill. The C.O. inspected "C" Company.	

WAR DIARY
or
INTELLIGENCE SUMMARY.

(Erase heading not required.) 12 Bn THE DURHAM LIGHT INFANTRY.

Army Form C. 2118.

Place	Date	Hour	Summary of Events and Information	Remarks and references to Appendices
NOORDPEENE	7/9/17		Inspection of feet, boots, socks etc of every man in the Battalion. A, B & D Co's training under Co Cmdrs. Inspection of C Co, also the billets, latrines etc by the Brigadier. The Bn loaned about 30 men to the farmers to help get in their beans.	AA
"	8/9/17		Battalion training. Co's under Co Cmdrs.	AA
"	9/9/17		Church parade in the morning and sports etc in the afternoon.	AA
"	10/9/17		Special practice of "Attacking strong points" in the morning. Practice by Battalion of "lining up on tapes" at night.	AA
"	11/9/17		Company parades for Bayonet fighting etc in the morning. Bayonet fighting etc in the afternoon. "B" & "D" Co's with 13th D.L.I. took part in Brigade practice attack.	AA
"	12/9/17		Lectures the disposal to be lectures to having Battalion moved by Route march to the STEENVOORDE AREA leaving abt 1-10 pm & arriving about 5-30 pm.	AA
	13/9/17			AA

Army Form C. 2118.

WAR DIARY
or
INTELLIGENCE SUMMARY. 12 BN THE DURHAM LIGHT INFT
(Erase heading not required.)

Instructions regarding War Diaries and Intelligence Summaries are contained in F.S. Regs., Part II. and the Staff Manual respectively. Title pages will be prepared in manuscript.

Place	Date	Hour	Summary of Events and Information	Remarks and references to Appendices
MURRUMBIDGEE CAMP.	14/9/17		The Battalion moved by route march to No 5 Area. MURRUMBIDGEE CAMP. Leaving at 7.30 am & arriving about noon.	A.A.
"	15/9/17		Bn in MURRUMBIDGEE CAMP. Inspection of Box respirators etc & general Bn training under Coy Cmdrs.	A.A.
	16/9/17		Battalion moved by route march to camp near HALLEBAST CORNER N.2.b.6.9.	A.A.
HALLEBAST CORNER CAMP.	17/9/17		Battalion bathed in baths at BURGOMASTER'S FARM. Inspection of motor transfer. disposal of Bomber for general training.	A.A.
"	18/9/17		Companies at the disposal of Coy Commanders. At G.O.C. in afternoon. Special clouded Coy Demonstration marched up to TORR TOP via BEDFORD HOUSE A & B companies marched to the trenches. (See operations attached). Remainder of Bn. moved to BEDFORD HOUSE leaving camp at 9.15 am and arrived on from there to TORR TOP later in the day.	A.A.
	19/9/17		Bn in attack as per special account attached. 69 Brigade on our left and 41st Division on our right.	A.A.
IN THE LINE	20/9/17 to 24/9/17		The whole of the Bn was relieved on the night of the 24 & 25 & proceeded to OTTAWA CAMP. ONTARIO CAMP	
	25/9/17		Battalion moved by route march to camp near WESTOUTRE in ARRAGON CAMP M.7.d.9.8.	A.A.

WAR DIARY
or
INTELLIGENCE SUMMARY

(Erase heading not required.) 12 Bn THE DURHAM LIGHT INFY.

Army Form C. 2118.

Place	Date	Hour	Summary of Events and Information	Remarks and references to Appendices
ARAGON CAMP	26/9/17		Inspection of Battalion by G.O.C. 23rd Division. 2 Drafts arrived 350 & 36 strong respectively. Games in afternoon.	00
"	27/9/17		C.O. inspected companies in battle order. Games in afternoon	00
RIDGE WOOD CAMP	28/9/17		Battalion moved by route march to RIDGE WOOD CAMP. leaving 9.30 am arriving about noon.	00
"	29/9/17		Battalion in RIDGE WOOD Camp N.5.C. (Sheet 28 Belgium) in reserve to 69th & 70 Brigades. Working & Carrying parties of 200 each. Supplies. Enemy dropped bombs in vicinity of camp. Several times during night.	/D
"	30/9/17		Same work. parte. Supplies — Bombs again dropped by Enemy Aircraft — no casualties.	/D

W. Hymsall Lt Colonel
C/o 12 Durham L.I.

12th. BATTALION THE DURHAM LIGHT INFANTRY.

Headquarters,

      68th. Infantry Brigade.

ACCOUNT OF ATTACK AND SUBSEQUENT OPERATIONS.

"A" and "B" Coys. moved up to TORR TOP on night of September 18th. They were employed on carrying parties on September 19th., and moved into assembly positions in the neighbourhood of JAM LANE at 2.30 a.m. on September 20th. These Companies moved off at ZERO behind 10th. and 11th. N.Fs. being held up by Strong Point and snipers in DUMBARTON WOODS and assisting to clear these. The Strong Point was held by 12 men At about 8 a.m., both Companies dug in about 20 yards in front of JASPER TRENCH in support to 10th. N.F. On night of Sept., 20th., they came under orders of 9th. Yorks. & Lancs. Regt. On night of Sept., 21st. orders were received to return to TORR TOP, but owing to a counter attack "A" Coy., was ordered forward and reinforced Yorks & Lancs in neighbourhood of BLUE LINE at about 7.30 p.m. About 9.30 p.m. situation became normal. "A" Coy., were ordered to return to JASPER TRENCH. During this counter attack "B" Coy. remained where they were to protect right flank if necessary. On morning of 22nd., about 6.30 a.m., the O.C. 9th. York & Lancs. ordered these Companies to return to TORR TOP in compliance with orders received the night before.

During the afternoon of the 22nd., and on the 23rd. and 24th. both Companies were employed in carrying to Dumps.

At 7 p.m., on Sept., 24th., both Companies were relieved by 16th. K.R.Rs. and returned to Camp.

"C" Company formed up, less Lewis Gun Sections, behind 13th. D.L.I. and moved at ZERO following 13th. D.L.I. to GREEN LINE where loads were dumped. Lewis Gun sections remained at TORR TOP until 10 a.m. when they moved to 13th. D.L.I. Adv. H.Q.

Remainder of Company made a total of three journeys carrying from JAM and JEFFERY DUMPS to GREEN LINE. On Sept., 21st., carrying parties made two more journeys and then returned to TORR TOP TUNNELS.

On night of 21st., Lewis Gun Sections were ordered to reinforce front line and right flank. One gun reached front line, two others were close to front line, and one was knocked out. At about 9 p.m. O.C.13th. D.L.I. ordered them to TORR TOP.

On the afternoon of Sept., 22nd., the whole Company moved to HOLY CORN dugout and dug in. At 4 p.m. on 23rd., the Company moved up to trenches near JASPER TRENCH and remained there until relieved at 4 p.m. on Sept., 24th., by Queens Regt.

"D" Company formed up near JAM LANE on night of 19/20th. and moved at ZERO behind 11th. N.F., up to JAM ROW and thence to JASPER DRIVE, encountering a strong point at J.20.a.1.2., which was successfully dealt with by a Sergeant and three men. The Company dug in near JASPER DRIVE.

Orders were then received to move to RED LINE, and a few minutes later, to reinforce 10th. N.F., in BLUE LINE, where they dug in on the right of "B" Coy., 10th. N.F. and remained there until 1 a.m. on 21st. when orders were received to return to RED LINE and one hour later to TORR TOP. At 6 p.m. on 22nd., they moved to LUCKY Dugout area, relieving "D" Coy. 11th. N.F., and acted as carrying party until relieved by 9th. York & Lancs. at 4.30 p.m. on 24th., inst.

(Sd). R. Iredale
Lieut-Colonel.
Commanding 12th.Bn.THE DURHAM LIGHT INFANTRY.

Sept., 26th., 1917.

WAR DIARY
or
INTELLIGENCE SUMMARY.

Army Form C. 2118.

Vol 25
12th Durham Light Infy.

Place	Date	Hour	Summary of Events and Information	Remarks and references to Appendices
RIDGE WOOD CAMP	1/10/17		Battalion in RIDGE WOOD CAMP. in DICKEBUSCH Reserve. 60 men were as carrying party at JACKDAW DUMP I.24.b.99. Enemy Aeroplanes bombed vicinity of camp several times during the night.	
"	2/10/17		Battalion was conveyed by busses to METEREN then marched to billets in BERTHEN AREA - arriving at 3.0 PM	
BERTHEN AREA	3/10/17		Battalion marched to THIEUSHOUK area, arriving at 3.0 PM	
THIEUSHOUK AREA	4/10/17		In tents at Thieushouk. Very wet day. Battalion would march at 6 PM - then fighting orders. Lewis gun instruction. Class in new Lewis Gun No 33495 Cpl E HALFORD killed by F.G.C.M. Battalion was under orders to move at ½ an hours notice.	
	5/10/17		The Battalion marched to CAESTRE entraining, detraining at DICKEBUSCH at 10.30 PM, marched off for camp at 11.20 PM but found no tent. Eventually Battalion settled down at midnight with one of Fort Skelton for the whole battalion - the camp	

2353 Wt. W2514/1454 700,000 5/15 D.D.&L. A.D.S.S./Forms/C.2118.

WAR DIARY or INTELLIGENCE SUMMARY.

Army Form C. 2118.

(Erase heading not required.)

(B'talion L.I.)

Place	Date	Hour	Summary of Events and Information	Remarks and references to Appendices
	5/9/17	(cont'd)	Was very muddy & slippery. Attached to 212th Brigade for the purpose of Supplying work parties for X Corps Signals.	10
	6/9/17		400 men supplies daily for X Corps Signals - burying Cable. Work hindered owing to wet weather.	M2
	10/9/17			
	11/9/17		Moved to RAILWAY DUGOUTS at 12 noon.	M2
	12/9/17		Work - preparing for trenches. Officers & NCO reconnoitre routes to Front Line.	M2
	13/9/17		The Battalion relieves 10' NF in right Subsector E of POLYGONE WOOD. Owing to hostile shell fire relief was not complete till dawn. Had 20 casualties going in. 9th Yorks on left, 11 NF on right.	M2
	14/9/17		The Battalion in the line. A constant enemy kept up on our Support line all night. Had 40 casualties.	M2
	15/9/17		Still in the line. Heavy shelling - an ordnance 20 casualties.	M2

WAR DIARY
or
INTELLIGENCE SUMMARY

Army Form C. 2118.

12 Durham L.I.

Place	Date	Hour	Summary of Events and Information	Remarks and references to Appendices
TRENCHES E.1. POLYGONE WOOD	16/10/17		In the Line. Enemy Shelling - still severe. One gun installing what appears - Enemy aeroplanes numerous & actively active - 19 Eprs were counted at one time flying low over our lines - firing into our trenches. When our Lewis guns engaged them - Relieved during the evening by 10" West Riding Regt. Relief complete at 8.45 p.m. Bay foot relief, under the circumstances. On relief proceeds to RAILWAY DUGOUTS.	M.S. M.S.
RAILWAY DUGOUTS	17/10/17		Battalion rested - Drummers clearing up & & equipment. Reorganising speciments after 2 total casualties in the line being 99 - 30 percent being Killed. Capt C. Power Smith + 2/Lt. Chapman wounded. The former severely.	M.S.
"	18/10/17		Resting in RAILWAY DUGOUTS. Received "marching orders" to relieve 10" West Riding Regt on night of 19/20	M.S.

WAR DIARY
or
INTELLIGENCE SUMMARY.

Army Form C. 2118.

12 Durham L.I.

Place	Date	Hour	Summary of Events and Information	Remarks and references to Appendices
RAILWAY DUGOUTS	19/6/17		The vicinity of RAILWAY DUGOUTS shelled. One man killed. Rained very heavily all day - consequently from a new working Sapt. Relieved 10th West Riding Regt in same Sect E. of POLYGONE Woods. Relief not complete until 7 am owing to shelling & guides losing their way. 13 D.L.I. on right, 9 YORKS on left.	AD
"	20/6/17		Shelling not so heavy. Back area came in for a good amount of shelling. One of our patrols captured a German Machine gun in a post out in front of our lines.	AD
"	21/6/17		Shelling fairly heavy all day. Enemy aeroplanes very active flying low over our positions, also firing "Very lights" at night so see movement on our front. Relieved by 15th D.L.I. Relief not complete tie daybreak — owing to guides knowing their way in the trenches by day only.	AD AD

WAR DIARY
or
INTELLIGENCE SUMMARY.
(Erase heading not required.)

12. Durham L.I.

Army Form C. 2118.

Place	Date	Hour	Summary of Events and Information	Remarks and references to Appendices
ST MARTIN AU LAERT	22/10/17		At 6 A.M. before relief was complete - An intensive Bing opens on our left - casualties received being shelling. Left THE BUND, entrained at 1-30 PM. Moved to the BUND. Detraining at ST MARTIN AU LAERT at 8.0 PM	no
	23/10/17		Battalion settling in Billets. Inspection of Rifles.	no
	24/10/17		Clothing and equipment etc. Parade 7am. A thorough cleaning up of Billets. 11 am Refitting of men clothing	no
	25/10/17		C.O.'s inspection in Billets. All men bathed at STOMER	no
	26/10/17		The superior G.O.C's inspection cancelled owing to wet weather. Handling arms & musketry exercises near camp	no
	27/10/17		7-30 AM to 8. am. Inspection of gas masks. Gun platoon drill 11 am Handling arms. 2 Pn Battalion extensive drill	no

WAR DIARY or INTELLIGENCE SUMMARY

Army Form C. 2118.

/2 Buckinghams 2/1

Place	Date	Hour	Summary of Events and Information	Remarks and references to Appendices
ST MARTIN AU LAERT	28/10/17		The inspection C in C. Inspection cancelled. The nurses training carries on.	/A
	29/10/17		The Battalion paraded for Brigade practice march past at Q.24 central (Sheet 27 A SE). The GOC traversed also inspected the Brigade.	/B
	30/10/17		The Battalion paraded at 8-45 A.M. for route march & recommenced returning. Returns - Strength 7 38 OR. arrived - all ranks. Battalion sports practices. 7 mules to Bellis about 12 noon. men 9. 19. — Speciale orig. 20 Lewis Gunners, 17 R. grenaders, 1 Signaller.	/C
	31/10/17		The Battalion was inspected with the Brigade by the Commander in Chief, Sir D. HAIG. at 11-20 A.M. at Q.24.Cent (Sheet 27 A SE). The C. in C. expressed his entire satisfaction & made the Battalion the best of what in its was centuries.	/D

R W Mugnifull Lt Colonel